IN HIS DAYS: THE LEGACY OF IDE GABRIEL NNOLIM EZEKWO

Dedication

I dedicate this book to my late father, Pa Gabriel Nnolim "Ndigiri" Ezekwo, and all the travelling teachers and catechists during his time in the 1900s. They were the forgotten missionaries who had the wisdom and courage to embrace Western education and Christianity when it was an abomination to do so in Igbo land. They put their lives and their families in danger and worked selflessly, trekking on jungle trails to spread the Gospel. Needless to mention that they received meagre pay for their efforts, however abundantly blessed by God for their sacrifice. They were the trailblazers.

These early teachers and catechists ran the schools as headmasters and the churches as priests, often under the same roof. There were no indigenous ordained priests at the time. The foreign missionaries were mostly in Lagos while they were in the trenches fighting for the spread of the Gospel in Igbo land. They did the work of present-day ordained priests and college principals and yet they are not mentioned in the history of the Church at Synod meetings. The mud school and church buildings they built for the early Church have been demolished, together with the foundation stones bearing their names.

This book is dedicated as well to all the towns in southeast Nigeria where Pa Gabriel Ezekwo evangelised, for providing him and his family safety, and the moral, spiritual and physical support that he so dearly needed to do his work. He returned home safely after fifty-one years of service as God's warrior.

I dedicate this book to all the past and present president-generals and executive officers of Umuchu Improvement Union (UIU) at home and at the branches that shared the vision of my father and helped in the establishment of UIU branches in all the major cities of Nigeria in the early 1900s.

This book is also dedicated to past and present Parochial Church Committee members of all Umuchu Church denominations, and Chairmen of St. Thomas (Ang.) Church Umuchu Men's and Women's General Meetings, for keeping the faith and maintaining the relevance of the Church and its mission in Umuchu community.

Finally, I dedicate this book to my siblings,

Comfort, Ozioma, Chinwe, Chijioke, Godson, Victor and Edith; to my wife, Ifeoma; my sons, Obiajulu and Chukwuemeka; my daughter-in-law, Becky; and my grandchildren, Gabriel and Gabriella.

Dad, I love you more than ever! Long live your legacy!! Long live your dynasty!!!

High Chief (Engr.) Samuel I. Ezekwo

Contents

Acknowledgements

In April 2017 I asked my attorney, Humphrey Osarenmwinda Esq., to help me find an investigative journalist who could research the life and career of my late father, so that I could use the information to write his biography. I had already interviewed two journalists. However, I needed a third person before selecting an investigator for the project. I was looking for a young, energetic professional who would see the project as an opportunity to enhance his or her career. I found that person in Mr. Ejiofo Umegbogu (JP).

Prior to engaging Mr. Umegbogu, I had visited nearly every community that my late father served in southeast Nigeria in 2016, during which time I gathered extensive information with which I created a road map for the research/investigation. So I readily provided Mr. Umegbogu with the road map, including too some collections of reference materials and publications that formed the bases of the research and insight into the life of the late Ide Gabriel Nnolim "Ndigiri" Ezekwo.

What followed was nearly three years of field research, in-depth review of relevant literature, and many interview sessions with people who could volunteer information on the legacies of Pa Gabriel Ezekwo. Not forgetting repeated visits to communities, churches and schools where Pa Gabriel lived and worked during his exemplary life as a pioneer teacher, visionary, evangelist, church administrator and social worker.

The first point of call was HRH Igwe Godson Ezechukwu OON, KSP, JP, an avid admirer of Pa Gabriel Ezekwo, and a man of undisputed and exemplary intellectual honesty. His attention to detail and willingness to provide any information available to him encouraged us to continue and complete this project.

Our investigator was a guest at the royal household of HRH Eze Joseph Mbamara, Obi-Aku of Amato-Amaraku for two days. It was a sumptuous and memorable stay. The warmth and hospitality extended to him by the Queen, Ugoeze Patience Mbamara, was particularly memorable.

There are other leaders of thought who were

consulted in the course of this research. They include Chief Eric Nwagboso, former Regent of Nawfija and Chairman of Ama-Ala Elders Council of the town; a former chairman of Orumba local government area, Chief (Hon.) Ben. Esiobu; the President-General of Nawfija, Mr Kinsley Onyeagba; and former president-general of UIU, Chief Chris Ezeoguine (Omeudo/Ogene Umuchu).

In addition, there are our assessors and all those who helped in directing our path towards retracing the footsteps of this great champion of community development and Christian missionary, in every community and church that was visited. These assessors and local agents are too numerous to mention here.

An unobtrusive impediment against fuller enquires into the life and times of early pioneers of Christian evangelism and Western civilisation has been the scant attention allocated to activities of missionary foot soldiers like Ide Gabriel Ezekwo.

They gave their all, yet received little. With faith, they climbed mountains and descended hills to establish churches and missionary outposts. Yet church records rarely give them credit for their exploits. Most records of church history or documents make reference to only the ordained clergy, with little or no emphasis to lay evangelists.

In the course of the investigation, we met very aged fellows who had also interacted with the subject of the investigation. From one community to another, their memory enriched our knowledge of the time and circumstances in which they lived, while illuminating our understanding of the life and times of Ide Gabriel Nnolim Ezekwo. They are simply too numerous to mention individually, and the substance of their interviews is contained in the exposition that follows.

The co-operation of those parish vicars towards the successful compilation of this biography must be acknowledged. As the research trail moved from one church to another in search of the giant footprints of the late itinerant worker, these priests opened wide their doors and called out the very aged members of their congregation who might be in possession of useful information concerning Pa Gabriel Ezekwo. There is no need to mention their names and the churches where we met them, because they may have been posted to some other churches by the end of this project.

It will be a great disservice if we forget to mention those who spent quality man hours to type or edit the manuscript. Thanks to Mrs. Amaka Ekwemba and O.A. Enweomuru (Ph.D.), respectively.

As much as we give due credit to other authors

consulted, we retain full responsibility for the editorial judgment contained in this book. *In His Days: The Legacy Of Ide Gabriel Nnolim Ezekwo* (A Biography) is not finality. It is just a modest attempt to probe beyond the known traditional layers of information available about the growth of Christianity in Igbo land, to stimulate further studies into the life of leading men and women whose activities affected the course of human history, and whose legacies are gradually being wiped away from living memory.

Finally, we wish to state with every sense of humility that this publication is not designed to mar the integrity, reputation or dignity of any person, group or community. Rather, it is to further enrich the history and identity of the people and communities mentioned herein. Therefore, any error of omission or commission as may be found in this book is unintentional and highly regretted.

High Chief (Engr.) Samuel I. Ezekwo
Mr. Ejiofo Umegbogu (JP)

Foreword

In His Days by Samuel Ezekwo and Ejiofo Umegbogu is a historical artefact that records the life and times of the late Ide Gabriel Nnolim Ezekwo. The author and co-author give a vivid historical antecedent of the legacy of Ide Gabriel Ezekwo and how he was used by God for church planting and growth in the old Owerri and Niger dioceses of southeast Nigeria.

I commend the authors for painstakingly researching the life of Ide Gabriel and coming up with information that will be very useful to church historians and those seeking to know how the gospel penetrated the regions of the old Owerri and Niger dioceses in their times.

Reading about the legacy of this missionary, philanthropist and educator as enunciated by the authors will ignite the passion of the younger generation to the service of dedication and commitment to God and humanity as exemplified by Ide Gabriel Ezekwo. As the authors put it, "Although they had a very minimal level of education when compared with pastors these days, those pioneers were very resolute, committed and convinced of their ecclesiastical vocation. They toiled day and night without much grease to their elbow." It was evident that they worked selflessly without expecting any pat on the back. Even when they were not appreciated nor rewarded by the church hierarchy, their zeal and enthusiasm to take the gospel of Jesus to the remotest parts of the land remains unrivalled.

The testimonies found in this book will definitely spur the reader to appreciate what God has done through men in the past, irrespective of their humble beginnings, and also evoke the spirit of selfless service with the understanding that God is the true rewarder of every man's labour. The life of this church worker and educator is an example to be copied in our time, especially to the younger generation who are always in the habit of seeking immediate gratification that may deny greater benefits to their generation.

Ide Gabriel Ezekwo was not only successful in his missionary enterprise but also in transforming his community. This historical record is full of inspiration that one can draw from to create a more impactful ministry in our time.

We therefore recommend this masterpiece for church and community leaders, students, lovers of history and the general public who would like to have an impact on their generation in a more definite way.

Rt. Rev. Sosthenes I. Eze, B. Engr (Hons), M.A.
Bishop, Anglican Diocese of Enugu North

Preface

I never planned in my wildest imagination to write a book during my retirement. As a practising engineer, I wrote dozens of technical papers and reports that targeted a limited select audience. I had never intended to write about any subject that would appeal to a wider audience. All that changed when I retired, returned to Umuchu from the United States of America in 2016 and assumed guardianship of my late father's legacy as his first son. The more I was involved in this noble project, the more it became apparent that I had an obligation to write a book about my father, Pa Gabriel Ezekwo.

This book had to be written for several reasons. First, no book on the history of Umuchu or any town where Pa Gabriel Ezekwo served can fully capture his accomplishments, as his service cuts across southeast

Nigeria. Second, the totality of his life has to be in a 'stand-alone' book in order for readers to appreciate his life and learn lessons from it. Third, research into his life, involving people that worked with him, and/or know about his life and career, with review of archives, was necessary to produce an authentic documentation of his life, thereby, separating the facts from fiction.

Growing up, I heard my father tell stories of his life and career in missionary work and community service. As a young boy, towards the latter part of my father's career, I witnessed him in action. But I never thought it would warrant writing a book, his biography. I remember one instance, which in hindsight made me think that my father wanted me to document his life's work. It was in August 1990, when I took my two young sons, Obiajulu and Chukwuemeka, to Umuchu for the first time to see my parents. During that visit, my father told me and my children stories of his life, and his accomplishments in Umuchu and beyond. He told us stories of how he converted communities to Christianity, built churches and schools, settled conflicts in communities, fearlessly told the truth to power, and trained/mentored people; and how he was always consulted in times of crises in Umuchu as the founder, first and longest-serving (ten years) president-general, and life patron of the UIU.

As if he wanted me to make sure that I kept all the facts, he went inside his bedroom and brought out a 24x24x24-inch mahogany safe box. He took out two books from the wooden box and told me to keep them for my records. Those two books were The History of Umuchu by S.A. Nnolim, published in 1952, and The Voice of Umuchu by Marius Nkwoh, published in 1964. He pointed out to me where he signed the books as if to authenticate them.

For some reason, I kept the books as a treasure for decades, as if I knew that one day the younger generations would try to rewrite history and deny Pa Gabriel Ezekwo credit for his contributions to mankind, especially in Umuchu town.

Upon my return from the United States of America, I noted with dismay that the younger generations have conveniently forgotten their history, especially that of the pioneers and founders of Umuchu who selflessly brought development to their communities. Worse still, some authors have written books that are intended to authenticate and codify the selective amnesia of the younger generations. The one that is most disturbing, erroneously described pre-1984 UIU as, "...market place for men... People walked into the meeting from different directions and at different times representing themselves and accountable to no one but themselves."

This assessment of pre-1984 UIU is completely unfounded and not supported by research. The sterling performance and integrity of dozens of president-generals and executive officers who have led the eighty-three-year-old organisation were diminished by this simple, disingenuous thought. Furthermore, it is an obvious contradiction to the history of Umuchu by S.A. Nnolim and The Culture-History of Umuchu from the Earliest Times to 1999 by Leo Nnoli that documented the opposite.

The more I observed the tendency to diminish the accomplishments of our pioneers and past heroes, the more I had flashbacks of my conversations with my father and how he insisted that I kept those books. Those books painted an indelible picture in my mind of how ancient Umuchu was organised before Pa Gabriel Ezekwo founded UIU. They established Pa Gabriel Ezekwo as the founder and father of a vibrant, progressive modern Umuchu with an effective government, as well as being one of the foremost missionaries that helped entrench Christianity in Umuchu and other communities in southeast Nigeria.

Pa Gabriel Ezekwo contributed immensely to many communities in southeast Nigeria. This makes it imperative that investigations and review of archives in far-away places in Imo State are undertaken. Since

I was very busy running the Ide Gabriel Nnolim Ezekwo Memorial Foundation, and trying to immortalise my late father in various communities that he served, I could not take on the task of the investigation and archives review. Therefore, I employed Mr. Ejiofo Umegbogu (JP), a respected historian and investigative journalist to visit all the communities where Pa Gabriel Ezekwo served in southeast Nigeria to conduct research on his life and his services in those communities.

After reading this book, you will discover that Pa Gabriel Ezekwo seemed to have found a model that worked, allowing him to plant and expand churches as well as bring development to many communities in southeast Nigeria, through his good rapport with host communities. Typically, he would organise town meetings/unions with community leaders who worked with the local churches to resolve conflicts among themselves and the Church. The town unions served as a feeder of pupils to the schools run by churches, in many cases offering scholarships to the poor. He embarked on programmes of extensive adult and children's education. Often, he conducted mass church weddings of tens of couples. With his wife, Mrs. Mercy Ezekwo (née Iloka), he introduced marriage counselling for wedded couples and the training of young women before their weddings.

The marriage counselling and training helped to improve the moral life of Christian couples, and increased family bonding among the faithful. He mobilised human and material resources from all members of the communities, bringing villagers, pagans and different church denominations together to construct church buildings, as well as other people-oriented projects.

Our research also sought to determine how, where and when Pa Gabriel Ezekwo learned this model, which he used so effectively in Umuchu and elsewhere as early as 1931, when he made the first attempt to establish the UIU. Some have speculated that he learned it from his travels and then applied it to his work at various places like Umuchu in 1937 and Amaimo in 1949. After reading this book, one cannot conclude that this was the case. The research of his life established that Pa Gabriel Ezekwo had travelled to Obosi, Nkwere-Opiegbe, Umuduru and Osina before 1931; however, there is no evidence that these towns had Improvement Unions at the time Pa Gabriel Ezekwo served in those places. Therefore, one can only conclude that he got the idea from his education by the European missionaries or that he articulated the model himself and applied it to facilitate his work.

This innovation has been adopted and adapted even to this day, in almost all the communities that came under the influence this great social crusader, teacher and church administrator, Ide Gabriel Nnolim Ezekwo… May his soul continue to rest in peace!!

Unfortunately, it is my opinion that present-day church leaders have not done much to protect the legacies of these saints-triumphant or showcase their contributions towards the spread of Christianity in the East of Nigeria.

This is evident in the deplorable manner that church administrators of these days mismanage church properties and documents left behind by those pioneers in the days of Pa Gabriel Ezekwo.

The effect is that our churches have lost the culture of recordkeeping. A few that tried to keep documents of past activities included only clergy and carefully excluded the remarkable efforts of lay workers. Consequently, catechists and other categories of lay church administrators are no longer finding a place in the annals of the church.

Church leaders in the days of Pa Gabriel Ezekwo maintained excellent records of activities, logbooks and diaries of events, from which their successes or failures could be evaluated. This evaluation would then serve as a signpost for the coming generation.

Let me take this opportunity to appeal to the leadership of the church of Nigeria, Anglican

Communion to urgently mandate that all churches submit their logbooks and other important archival documents to the dioceses, where there should be an established central library that can safeguard these documents as a resource material for future uses.

High Chief (Engr.) Samuel I. Ezekwo

Introduction

The setting of this book is the ancient Igbo kingdom of Umuchu in Aguata Local Government Area, Anambra State, in the southeastern part of Nigeria.

The subject, Ide Gabriel Nnolim Ezekwo, was born in Umuchu in 1888 and accepted Christianity and Western education in 1913 around the time the European adventurers were just establishing footprints in the hinterland after successfully converting the Igbos in the coastal areas to Christianity and introducing a Western education and way of life.

As this book conveys the opinions of the time and the people in this community, not every reader may share these ideas. The author urges the reader to keep in mind that these views are specific to the community and cultural background described in the book.

The author was born before Nigerian independence. During the author's childhood (and primary education) much of the history of Nigeria was written from a European perspective. During his secondary education, works by Nigerian historians started shedding light into the period spanning the pre-colonial, colonial, and post-colonial eras with less European influence.

As this book is written from a Nigerian perspective, the views expressed in it reflect those of the author's community in Nigeria, and as such, may not reflect the opinions of every reader. The author hopes that this brief introduction serves to help worldwide readers understand the perspective from which this book has been written.

The aim of this book is to showcase the author's late father's contributions to society to a worldwide audience, and demonstrate how his father, alongside his contemporaries, can be immortalised and celebrated.

Chapter One

The Man in His Environment

By the twilight of the nineteenth century, nations of Europe were beginning to signify interests in the areas that were referred to as the black man's continent. An era that has gone down in history as the period of scramble for Africa.

Their interests were diverse and varied, depending on the foreign policy direction of the nation states. These included, but were not limited to, the expansion of economic interests, military influence and cultural extension, all aimed at building stronger empires through imperialism. The major instruments of advancing their overseas strongholds were Gold, Guns and God.

European powers including Britain, Germany, France, Belgium and Portugal among others had assembled in Berlin to partition Africa amongst themselves, purportedly to avoid a possible clash of interests between them, in their quest to establish influence in the 'dark continent'.

This was the period when European anthropologists, merchants and journalists were writing what could best be described as esoteric reports and negative descriptions of Africa, its culture and its people.

Based on these negative fairy tales by so-called explorers and merchants, black Africa, and indeed Africans, bore a kind of stigma of inferiority and exploitation, and were regarded as the 'white man's burden'. So-called advanced Western societies believed that they bore the moral obligation to carry the blessings of their own religion and civilisation to the supposed 'backward' peoples. English statesman and leading exponent of imperialism Joseph Chamberlain declared in 1893 that "it is our duty to take our share in the work of civilisation in Africa". Supporting this view, former British prime minister Benjamin Disraeli averred that "God has made us adept in government that we may administer government among savage and servile people".

With this mindset, the imperialists sought to establish their influence on the territories awarded to them by the Otto von Bismarck-led Berlin conference, through the policy of effective occupation.

All the geographical areas extending from the

north of the River Niger to the southern hinterlands, and stretching from the south of Lake Chad down to the Bight of Biafra, fell within the jurisdictional mandate of the then British Empire.

Merchant ships were sent out to establish trading posts under the royal charter, followed by colonial administrators to establish effective control of the people, and military gunboats to subdue by brute force people who might try to resist their commercial and colonial interests.

As a matter of deliberate policy, a voyage contingent would necessarily include people representing these three major interests' areas, namely: Imperial Trade, Colonial Administration and Christian Evangelism.

The first and most remarkable illustration of this fact was the 1854 Niger expedition led by Dr. William Baikie, of which representatives of the various interests constituted the company. In 1857 the company docked at Onitsha river port. They met with the king and chiefs of Onitsha. Prof. Kenneth Dike recorded thus, "Dr. W.B. Baikie, leader of the expedition, spoke for the British government, while Captain Grant dealt with commercial matters and Rev. S.A. Crowther led the missionary group."[1]

On 27 July 1857, the first church service was held with about 400 converts in attendance, marking the commencement of Christian evangelism in the lower Niger territories.

Another treaty, dated 12 October 1863, was signed between Onitsha and Great Britain "for the suppression of slave trade, to prevent Human sacrifices and to encourage legitimate trade."[2]

The British had a strategy of including pastors and clergy, otherwise known as missionaries, in their voyages, whose duty was to evangelise the pagan population, and with the responsibility to be the forerunners of British colonial administration in those areas.

The imperialists encouraged their missionary counterparts to move into the interior to introduce Christianity, open up trade relationships and educate the indigenous people who would form the human resource base of the colonial administration and the Church.

It was during this early stage in the age of imperialism that the little Nnolim Ezekwo was born.

By the time he was born in 1888, the Church Missionary Society (CMS) had already established churches and missionary outposts in the Riverine areas of Aboh in the present-day Ndokwa area of Delta State, and Osamali in the present Ogbaru area of Anambra State, while Onitsha was chosen as the centre for the spread of Christendom in the east. From here, the early missionaries were already making considerable in-roads into the neighbouring Obosi and Ogidi communities.

It's worthy of note that the early missionaries and explorers had to negotiate and sometimes forcefully subjugate the various communities of people existing in the lower Niger, because apart from a few towns that had achieved the status of a kingdom before the coming of the white man, most Igbo people existed independently in small kindred or clan groups owing to their fundamentally republican nature. As such, the community was too fragmented to have mustered any meaningful resistance to the colonial intrusion.

Such was the case at that period with the territory that is now known and referred to as Umuchu, in Aguata Local Government Area of Anambra State, when the family of Nze Ezekwo Ezeunara and Madame Ihuoma Ezeunara (née Achugamonye) of Umuezeukwu kindred in Umuojogwo village, Ogwugwu people, heralded the birth of Nnolim, who was later to become a frontrunner in the march towards Christian missionary evangelism in most communities in the hinterland areas of the eastern part of Nigeria.

Rev. Ajayi Crowther with a few other expatriates and freed slaves worked tirelessly to establish strong foundations for Christian evangelism. The Ezeunara family of Umuezeukwu kindred in Umuojogwo village welcomed the birth of a son who not only built on the Christian foundation, but radically advanced the course of Christian evangelism, Western education and community administration in the east of Nigeria.

By this period in history, Ogwugwu, also known as Imenano, existed as a distinct community of people who claim a common patricidal ancestry to a progenitor called Ezeledoranya. As is typical with every traditional Igbo community, traditions of origin are naturally associated with most if not all indigenous Igbo groupings. While some of these traditions have some degree of empirical evidence to prove them, most of them still rest in the realm of speculative history of an undocumented past, passed on from generation to generation and only written in the memory of village elders. It is posited by G.I. Jones that "the average Igbo village or even clan believes itself to be the descendant of a common ancestor whose sons begat either the village sections or the village subsection."[3]

In the case of the Ogwugwu people, there is a recurring traditional story that a certain man called Ezeledoranya from Urualla area in the present Orlu region had migrated alongside his wife Ederegwom and took refuge at a valley called Ogwugwu. There, the couple begot four sons, Umeilo, Umeogu, Ojogwo and Ojum. Their descendants are the present Umumilo, Umumeogu, Umuojogwo and Umuojum, being the four clans that constituted the village that grew around Ogwugwu Valley, also known as Imenano (meaning 'four conceptions').[4] They were later merged with three other settlements, namely Amihe, Osete and Ogu, to form what is today known as Amanasaa, literally meaning 'Seven Villages'. The lumping together of these village groups was purposely done, based on geographical and administrative reasons.

It is noteworthy that this merger was done not just because of geographical contiguity and administrative convenience but also for the purposes of better economic and security integration. Hence, the semi-autonomous villages were grouped into one administrative quarter called Amanasaa, together with two other similar quarters, namely Ihitenato and Okpu-na-Achalla, to form a confederacy that is today known as Umuchu.

According to Leo Nnoli, some of the factors considered to have necessitated the formation of the confederal union include, but are not limited to, the need for closer collaboration in matters of maintaining internal security, warding off external aggression and increasing the scope of socio-economic interdependence already existing among the semi-autonomous republican units.

In summary, Umuchu town is divided into three administrative quarters, namely Amanasaa, Ihitenato and Okpu-na-Achalla, with twelve villages, which include Ugwu-Akwu, Umugama, Ozara-Akukwa, Ogu, Osete, Umubuilo, Umubuogu, Umuojogwo, Umuojum, Amihe, Ibughubu and Achalla, as well as numerous kindred groupings that are too numerous to mention.

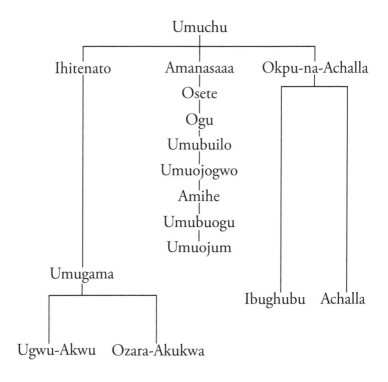

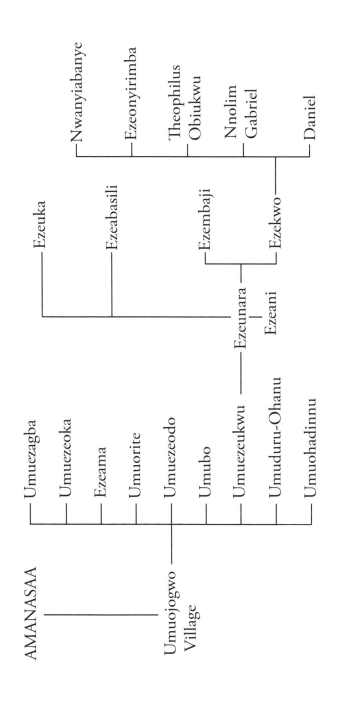

The source of the name 'Umuchu' is shrouded in myth and legend, just like names of many other Igbo communities or towns.

Firstly, it is believed that it was derived from the name of a river called Uchu River, which criss-crossed most villages in the town. Umu-uchu ordinarily means offspring or products of Uchu River. Just like the name 'Nigeria' was derived from 'Niger area', meaning the land and people living in the area surrounding the River Niger.

Concomitant to this legend was the tradition of origin as was documented by S.A. Nnolim and reconfirmed by the narrative of a ninety-five-year-old Ezeafulukwe Obidike as documented by Leo Nnoli[5], to the effect that the name originated from the day the confederacy was formed or the day of unification of the different kindred and villages that were, ab initio, independent of each other. There was, and there is still, a common myth of origin that associated the Umuchu with a certain ritual consummated by an oath or covenant between the elders that represented the constituent villages that gathered at a venue that is today known as Nkwo-Uchu to discuss and agree on the basis of their union.

After agreeing on certain fundamentals for their peaceful coexistence as a people in what seems like a re-enactment of the biblical injunction in Exodus

24:1, the elders prayed and offered sacrifices to God. Two powerful sacrificial packages were prepared, believed to have been sealed with the oral and blood oaths of the representative heads of various groups therein assembled. The two wraps were hypothetically called 'Uchu' and 'Ichu'.

Some of the fundamental principles agreed include the oath of allegiance not to engage in any form of conflict with one another but to continually work for peace and unity among the confederating units, in the spirit of brotherhood and solidarity.

They further agreed as follows:

1 Ihite quarter, headed by Ugwuakwu village, is recognised as the head of the great union.

2 That the confederacy be known as Umuchu.

3 A Council of representatives from all the villages is constituted. This council meets on Nkwo market days to discuss common issues affecting the union.

4 All norms, customs, rules and regulations governing the confederation should be stipulated and streamlined.

5 That an annual festival be instituted in order to sustain the relationship bond among them.

One of the packages, 'Ichu', believed to be the carrier of bad omens, negativities or calamities, which the assembly prayed God to take away from the unified communities thenceforth, was said to have been taken away and dispatched to the spiritual realm via a nearby lake, which is now known as Uchu Lake (probably a corruption of Ichu as a result of the constant usage of Uchu, which was the antidote of Ichu). The other consignment, 'Uchu', packaged to attract favours, good will, unity, peace and progress for the confederate union, was also sent forth to the world unknown by burying it at that place of meeting now called the Uchu shrine located around Nkwo-Uchu market. This popular account, and perhaps the most acceptable oral tradition among the people, was highlighted in the first written history of the town that was put together by S.A. Nnolim in 1952.

In Igbo traditional worldview, such spiritual packages of great sacrificial significance to the existence of a people must necessarily come in double packages, Oath (Iyi) and Antidote (Ndagbu-Iyi), to depict the divine order of creation big and small, male and female, black and white etc., and in obedience of the ultimate nature of the universe as espoused by philosophers in metaphysics who hold that all real entities have both essence and existence, form and matter, positive and negative force; and, logically, thesis and antithesis, or better still, blessings and curses under the Abrahamic covenant.

Hence, that act of fraternal entanglement brought together the hitherto ancestrally and culturally diverse settlements into a single symphony of brotherhood, which developed a particular spiritual character and a common sense of understanding that became the soul of the union. This soul came to be the unique property of every citizen, something that is inherent in the individual, something that one is born with, and will presumably take with one to the next life. In fact, like a generic spiritual personality, which Corbett Joe described as "a property of communal solidarity, love and compassion for one another."[6]

In agreement with this, Raymond Arazu explained the curses and blessings formula as "a treaty that stands wholly within the realm of sacred law."[7] The curses and blessings in the testaments are treated as the actions of the gods and it enumerated the same sort of things as those to be found in Holy Bible at Deuteronomy 28.

The point made here is that this covenant not only gave the town a common spiritual identity, but also gave birth to a union of many clans, founded by different ancestral figures.

Another source and probable meaning of the name 'Umuchu' was expounded by Igwe Godson Ogbunanwa Ezechukwu OON, the paramount ruler of the community, to the effect that the original founder of Umuchu was a legendary figure from Aro called Ezedike from Amankwu village in Arochukwu, who was a cousin to Izuogu, who is also said to have founded other settlements in the present-day Aguata and Orumba – such as Ndikelionwu, Ndi-okpalaeze, Ndi-okoro, Ndiowu, Ajali etc. – Ezedike came with his wife named Echu. They settled in an area that is now known as Umuchu and were blessed with five male children – Ogbu (Umuezeogbu), Akwu (Ugwuakwu), Agama (Umugama), Ohu (Umu-ohu) and Aku (Ozara-Akukwa).[8]

He explained that "to distinguish children from the ones born to Ezedike in Amankwu-Arochukwu (before his migration) they were called Umuechu as was the practice in those days of polygamy and numerous children from the same father, to name children after their mother's name."[9] The erudite paramount ruler contended that it was the name 'Umuechu' that was later to be corrupted as Umuchu.

At best, this conjecture could be grouped alongside other folktales that could be collectively evaluated as a signpost that may give a clue to the origin of the name given to the amalgamating communities today known as Umuchu.

Igwe Godson Ezechukwu concluded, and quite frankly too, that the town as it exists today was an amalgam of various settlements, which were originally founded by some ancestral figures that migrated to the area from other places, following different waves of migration, such ancestral figures as Ezeledoranya (from Uruala), Ezeayika (from Ikeduru), Ezedike (from Arochukwu) and so on. These ancestors, with their descendants, settled in the area and founded the various clans that later came together to form the larger town that is now known as Umuchu.

Be that as it may, Umuchu as a name and as a people had long existed with rich socio-cultural, religious, economic and even political heritage.

Several Afrocentric writers have romanticised the advanced civilisation of most indigenous African peoples before the advent of Europeans. This is in opposition to the Eurocentric writings of Western anthropologists and historians, to the effect that Africa does not have an enviable record of existence and which tended towards demonising the continent as dark and savage. By the twilight of the nineteenth century, the people had evolved a body of rich cultural norms and practices just like any other Igbo society before their contact with the outside world.

Part of the highly advanced and often complicated cultural practice that was mostly interwoven with religious observances includes the elaborate process of initiation of adult men into the Ozo title.

The journey to the Ozo traditional title in

Umuchu commences with 'Igbuichi', or facial scarification, of those who aspire to be enlisted into the group of titled men. Igbuichi, and its female version known as 'Itumbibi' or scarification of the lower abdomen, ankles and arms, was evidently part of the remnant of their Nri ancestry. This cultural artistry, coupled with the existence of the popular Nri symbol of justice, 'Ofo', domiciled with Ogu village of Amanasaa quarter, are anthropological proofs of an ancestral link to Nri.

Special tattoo itinerant craftsmen from Oraeri or Nri were usually invited to perform this task. It is noteworthy that descendants of these craftsmen later settled in the area and were assimilated as citizens of the town.

For the men, it was a preparatory step towards acquiring a title, while to the female folk, it was part of the ceremonies marking the entry of the adolescent girl into adulthood and then seen as being ready for marriage.

Marriages in those days involved a spectacular process. There are identifiable stages a girl had to undergo before the society would permit her to live with a man as husband and wife. There were, Ntutuisi, Ahiahi, Okpuazu, Isiego and Isiokpoko. These stages involved stylish plaiting of the hair signifying adulthood; belly scarification, to show that the maiden was now mature enough to bear children; body tattooing, with local make-up items like Ufie, Edo, Otanjele and so on, to exhibit the maiden's beauty; as well as teeth carving (Ikpoke-eze) to enhance the maiden's attractiveness.

The eighty-five-year-old Mr. Christian Ezekwo explained that in the olden days, "it was a big festival, which every young boy and girl must undertake before marriage. During such ceremonies, boys were given little facial marks (not as pronounced as those for the Ozo title), while the girls were also given such marks on their torsos. Then, the celebrants were decorated with good perfumes, body oil (like Uhie, Edo, Otangele, Uli, etc.) and laced with waist bands (Jigida and ringing bells), as well as new fabrics and beads with good hair styles. They would march through the major village centre, dancing and accepting cheers from people.

Young men would use the occasion to indicate their interests/intention to marry and complete the marriage process."[10]

Every traditional Igbo society during the pre-colonial era had some handful of periodic feasts and festivals it celebrated, and Umuchu could boast of quite a number of them.

Feasts are acts and observances that members of any given society hold very dear to their heart, while festivals are periodic ceremonies that any society holds at high esteem, as a necessary part of their social interactions.

By the late nineteenth century the different quarters that constituted Umuchu community had several traditional feasts and festivals that they celebrated as part of their culture.

Ogwugwu people of Amanasaa quarter has cultural festivals like Ala, Ulo-Isiogwu, etc.

Each of these cultural festivals had its own coordinator in the person of a chief priest, who was superintendent of such festivities, and was performed at a particular venue, usually at a shrine specially designated for that purpose.

There were, however, three very important traditional festivities that brought all the people of Umuchu together. These were festivals that the entire community celebrated jointly. These were the throwing of pumpkin leaves (Ituonu-ugbogulu), the seed yam festival (Itu-Mkpuluji) and the new yam festival (Iriji-ofuu).

Without going into the nitty-gritty of the meaning and circumstances surrounding those celebrations, it is imperative to note the significance of these traditional festivities.

Perhaps the most important was Itu-Mkpuluji festival. This was when every adult male in Umuchu had to bring a tuber of yam to the inner sanctuary of the Uchu shrine as a sacrificial offering at the beginning of a new lunar calendar.

This great festival seemed to be the most significant to both the individual and collective life of the people of this area, largely because it bore huge socio-political and spiritual importance to their existence.

Socio-politically, it was a time for a community head count. As a patriarchal society, it was a time to take the census of all living adult males who must make themselves available at the shrine to be counted by offering a tuber of yam to the gods of the land, under the watchful eyes of the two revered high priests from Ugwuakwu and Osete villages, and in the full glare of another six elderly representatives of the three main administrative quarters. The number of yam tubers presented by each village was a satisfactory indicator of their demography. Of course, the population strength of a people determines its military might and its agro-economic contribution to the confederacy or, generally, its viability as a community.

Spiritually, this occasion was a re-enactment of the oath of allegiance taken by the founding fathers of the union during the historic amalgamation. By selecting twelve tubers from the pyramid of yams that was gathered each year, which the chief priest roasted and ate as a sin offering for each new moon, the community maintained a twelve-month lunar year.

As pointed out by Leo Nnoli, "the eating of the last yam tuber signalled the end of the year for the town, thus marking the commencement of the next Itu-Mkpuluji annual census festival."[11]

Traditionally, at the fourth sacrificial burnt yam offering, the chief priest announces the second-most important feast, called Ituonu-ugbogulu.

Ituonu-ugbogulu was celebrated around the months of April/May, when the chief priest of Uchu shrine would lead the rest of the people in praying for a successful crop-farming season, using the pumpkin leaves and seedlings as a totem representing other crops and vegetables, which were generally planted by the people at subsistent level.

Another feast that was of great significance in Umuchu pre-colonial society was the Iwaji festival, celebrated around the month of July/August every year like most Igbo traditional societies. This involved the offering of a great sacrifice to God for a successful planting and harvesting season. This was followed by bounteous merriment that is marked with great pomp and circumstance after which people can freely sell, buy and eat yams.

The new yam festival involving the commemorative first yam exhibition and eating, as well as so many other highly significant socio-cultural and religious observances, took place at the Nkwo-Uchu Market Square.

This, in effect, is indicative of the historical fact that the Nkwo-Uchu square has been, and is still, of great significance in the collective existence of the people. Evidence abounds that the area was the centre of all socio-cultural, religious and economic activities of the time.

Just like every other indigenous people in the eastern part of Nigeria, agriculture was the mainstay of their economy. As the primary occupation of any pre-literate society, agriculture formed the basis of all commercial and economic activities. Individuals might acquire other skills or craftsmanship, but they maintained their subsistence farming ventures. Such other trades like wine-tapping, pottery, animal husbandry, etc. did not vitiate people's primary occupation, which was subsistent agriculture. Thus, farming was the people's dominant source of livelihood, food supplies and goods for exchange at the local markets.

As highlighted earlier, there were other markets in the town apart from Nkwo-Uchu. They included Afor-Ibughubu, Afor-Achalla, Eke-Ubo and Eke-Ebelebe. However, Nkwo-Uchu remained the most central and invariably the boiling point or point of convergence for almost all economic, socio-political and even religious activities.

A barter system of commercial transaction was the dominant mode of exchange of goods and services, even though the people were also familiar with the use of cowries during this pre-literate era in the history of Umuchu.

In effect, this was the peasant society that existed during the days of Nnolim Ezekwo.

The birth of a newborn in Umuchu of those days, as ever, heralded a great joy in the family. It was seen as a fulfilment of the universal mandate to procreate in order to sustain human existence on Earth. This is in line with the divine directive, "Go ye into the world and multiply."

As soon as a child was born it was normal for the parents to engage the service of diviner, whose duty it was to consult the gods and ascertain the child's destiny. This is the essence of the Ilu-Agwu ritual that was usually performed in early life. It involved the making of a sacrifice of food and drinks to the guardian angel or the supernatural forces or spirits that control every individual.

Someone's Agwu is thought to have a considerable influence in the shaping of one's destiny, as well as the individual's progress or otherwise, in this physical plain.

However, owing to the belief that everyone has his own "chi" as epitomised by his or her individual spirit-god called Agwu, the birth of twins was therefore thought to be unacceptable, as multiple birth presupposes the idea that the twins possess one destiny or are controlled by one "chi". This belief formed the foundational thought-system that gave rise to the idea of the killing of twins in Igbo cosmology, as was experienced in almost all traditional African societies during the pre-colonial era.

After eight days or two market weeks, the newborn child was circumcised, whether male or female. This is a striking similarity between traditional Igbo society and the Jewish culture that is rooted in the Abrahamic injunction as contained in Genesis 1710-14, the only difference being that most Igbo communities including Umuchu also subjected their females to the solemn rite of circumcision.

A post-natal nursing period of eight weeks from the day the woman was delivered of the baby was customarily observed, at the end of which the nursing mother would perform her first outing ceremony at the market square.

This prevailing socio-cultural milieu was re-enacted in 1888 following the birth of little Nnolim into the family of Ezekwo and Ihuoma, of Ezeunara extended family, of Umuezeukwu sub-group, Umuojogwo kindred, Ogwugwu village within Amanasaa quarter in Umuchu, of present-day Aguata local Government Area of Anambra State in the southeastern part of the Nigeria federation, Sub-Saharan Africa.

Chapter Two

In Search of the Golden Fleece

Ezekwo Ezeunara and Ihuoma Ezeunara (née Achugamonye) followed the precedents of their progenitors in nurturing the infant according to the accepted social norms and values of the society in which it pleased the Almighty creator and supreme architect of the universe to place the young Nnolim. He had a normal social life for an adolescent of his time and place, with good friends cutting across both sexes.

Alongside his two elder brothers, Ezeonyirimba and Theophilus, they made the effort to raise him in a typically modest African traditional setting, until the unfortunate demise of both parents, first his father and later his mother. Growing up during this period no doubt became increasingly challenging, especially for a young lad who had lost his parents to the cold hands of death and had come under the care of his elder brother, Ezeonyirimba.

The vagaries of the life of an orphan in a time when this part of the world was undergoing tremendous sociological changes – such as the forceful emasculation of indigenous territories by European intruders in a bid to entrench their supremacist colonial administration, insecurity in most Igbo communities following the Abam war menace, and the debilitating escapades of Aro slave raiders, as well as a high mortality rate as a result of several incurable diseases, especially the chicken pox influenza – were the predominant features of the society in which the young Nnolim grew up.

At this time also, the stories of missionary successes in the coastal areas were beginning to filter into the hinterland communities. It is a natural consequence that humans respond to these environmental stimuli.

The tales of British gunboat diplomacy, and the establishment of schools, churches and hospitals in the late nineteenth century and early twentieth century, were propelling factors for the migration of people towards the coastal communities. Following this wave of migration, those areas started acquiring a cosmopolitan nature and were fast beginning to be viewed as cities.

By 1913, the young Nnolim was no longer satisfied with the challenges of living in a peasant society without parents to provide the soothing balm for most of his life's struggles or guide the thoughts of his adolescent mind, which was already brooding with inquisitiveness. Nnolim decided to take a plunge into the world unknown.

In his quest for the golden fleece of knowledge and the possibility of a better life, he trekked through the dangerous bush paths, meandering through perilous forest for several days, and finally landed at Obosi, near Onitsha, in southeast Nigeria. His stay at the area brought him into contact with foreign missionaries and indigenous Christians at the oldest prefabricated church, east of the Niger, now known as St. Andrew's Church. The component structures of the church are said to have been fabricated abroad, shipped into the country, and fixed on ground around 1880.

This adventure was cut short by lack of financial support to engage in any meaningful venture or commence Western education, because of an obvious lack of sponsorship as a result of the secrecy that shrouded his movement to the area. By the time he returned to his hometown, he was already favourably disposed to the white man's religion and ways of life.

Nnolim was later to recount how he met the first Igbo man to be ordained a Reverend in the CMS,

George Nicholas Anyaegbunam, who advised him to be patient and allow God to direct his ways.

Like a prophesy, Rev. Anyaegbunam told him that all you needed was a lever (in the form of support) and a little room (in terms of chance) to put it under, in order to lift any object, however heavy it might be. Convinced that every success begins with a little help from someone else, Nnolim returned to his elder brother's care and support, waiting for better opportunity to re-launch him.

That opportunity came knocking again in 1916, when some illustrious sons of Umuchu, who possessed the requisite clout and resources, successfully explored the possibilities and actually attracted the CMS mission to the town. Nnolim did not fail to take due advantage of that opportunity to actualise his desire.

Other people had different causes to migrate or at least visit these fast-developing towns and their adjoining communities. Some of the discernable reasons for population increase in the coastal towns included pursuit of Western education; opportunities in the emerging British public service system; need for orthodox Medicare for some disease outbreaks like influenza; the growing spate of Christian evangelism; the increasing level of trading and commercial activities on legitimate goods along the coastal lines;

and so many other reasons that may be related or ancillary to the aforementioned, not forgetting those running away from their local communities as fugitive to some negative customary law and practices.

As mentioned above, the people of the hinterland had serious need for medical services – people who could not cure their diseases by traditional/local medical remedies like roots and herbs went to the hospitals run by the missionaries to seek cure.

Within the first decade of the twentieth century, one Emenike Oduagu Orachusi of Ihite quarters had need to take his ailing wife to Iyi-Enu Hospital in Ogidi, near Onitsha, for treatment of a uterus infection she had contracted after a stillbirth. The impressive medical attention that patients received at the health facility, which was managed by CMS health workers, led Mr. Orachusi to make a return trip to the health facility, with his ailing brother, named Agbalafo, who had contracted the influenza disease that was prevalent during the First World War.

Iyi-Enu Hospital, located eight kilometres east of Onitsha along the Onitsha-Enugu Trunk A road, Anambra State, was originally established in Ozalla area of Onitsha in 1907 by the CMS's Niger Medical Mission, where the CMS carried on the healing ministry of Christ through caring for the sick, the suffering and the dying.[12]

Mr. Orachusi's disposition to embrace the new religion was greatly increased because of the treatment and subsequent recovery of his sick relatives. He made several requests to attract the missionaries to Umuchu, for the benefit of having a similar hospital established closer home.

As one of the foremost missionary health centres of that time, and arguably, the centre of excellence in orthodox medical practice in the whole of eastern Nigeria, it was common to see patients brought from far and wide by their loved ones. Most of these sick persons suffered from all kinds of serious health challenges that were deemed to have gone beyond the potency of trado-medicine.

His several requests caught the attention of the then Archdeacon of Onitsha, Rev. G.T. Basden, who permitted missionaries based in Nnewi and Ekwulobia to visit the town every Eke market day, to hold an open-air evangelism. Many were converted to Christianity as a result of this regular outdoor preaching that started sometime in 1916.

Following the increase in the number of converts, it became necessary to have a resident church teacher, who would undertake the task of administering the growing 'Body of Christ'. Through the combined efforts of Emenike Oduagu Orachusi, Chief Ezeanyim Ezenwaka and Chief Umeoduagu

Anyida, the CMS, in 1917, drafted one church teacher, Mr. Isaac Okonkwo, an indigene of Ufuma. To ensure the security of the church teacher, he was placed under the protection of the native court in Isuofia.

Mr. Okonkwo was later joined by two missionaries from the West Indies, namely Rev. L. Llewellyn and Rev. Cecil Brown.

With the coming of the two expatriate missionaries, the work of CMS evangelism commenced in Umuchu, leading to the construction, completion and dedication of the first church building. The church that was built with mud and roofed with thatches was erected in a stretch of land donated by Emenike Orachusi and other families. The building project lasted between 1917 to late 1918, followed by the dedication service, during which the church assumed the name St. Thomas CMS Church.

As recorded by the first ordained Anglican clergy from Umuchu, the late Archdeacon Christopher A. Mbonu, the first adult baptism was conducted in St. Thomas Church on 8 December 1918 by Rev. Cecil Brown.[13]

Available records of the pioneer converts that were baptized in Umuchu show that ten people formed the nucleus of the budding Christian community in the town. Among them was Nnolim Ezekwo, who by virtue of the doctrine of Christian baptism was given the name 'Gabriel'.

The thirty-year-old Gabriel Nnolim Ezekwo was baptised alongside other adults, including John Onwuzuligbo Nwankwo, James Onyedibe Okonkwo, David Umunwa Ezenwata, Daniel Okeke Nnoli, Simon Igwilo Anyora, Josiah Okonkwo Mbamalu, Hezekiah Ezealua Uneozo, Josiah Agodi Emenike and John Abalofo Orachusi.

According to Christian theology, by the sacrament of baptism Nnolim became a new creature in the body of Christ (the church) with Gabriel as his Christian nomenclature. Thus, Nnolim has become a priest, a king and a prophet, through the canonical anointing with chrism oil and the solemn proclamation by a servant of God (Rev. Brown), while the congregation bore witness. Thenceforth, he is expected not to be ashamed to confess his faith in Christ-crucified, with the obligation to fight under God's banner, against sin, the world and the devil, and to become Christ's faithful soldier and servant until the end of his earthly life.

Undisputedly, baptism remains the foundational step in Christian discipleship. As commanded by Jesus Christ himself in Matthew 28:19, "Go therefore and make disciples of all the nations, baptising them in the name of the Father and Son and the Holy Spirit."

This calls to mind also the statement of St. Peter the Apostle: "Repent, and let each of you be baptised in the name of Jesus Christ, for the forgiveness of your sins and you shall receive the gift of the Holy Spirit". It was indeed a turning point in the life of the new converts.

Fired up by the light of baptism and the flame of the Holy Spirit received, these pioneer Christian converts were poised to pick up the gauntlet and disseminate the message of salvation through Christ-crucified.

But first, they must conquer ignorance by embracing enlightenment, which Western education could offer through learning the art of reading and writing. Education was a necessary ingredient needed to spice up the zeal of the new believers and very vital in equipping them for the task of propagating the gospel to the rest of their kith and kin.

As was the norm in that era, fresh converts were enrolled in elementary schools, established and manned by missionaries.

Christianity fully berthed in Umuchu in 1918 and education landed in Umuchu in the same year, by the establishment of the CMS Primary School within St. Thomas Church premises. Gabriel Nnolim Ezekwo and other believers formed the pioneer class of the school.

Different studies have fully demonstrated that in establishing themselves on the Atlantic coast of tropical Africa in what later became Nigeria, and in penetrating the hinterland, the Christian missions relied on, among other methods, the attractions of Western education. Thus, by conceiving of education as a major bait of proselytisation, the missions had a very narrow view of education for the indigenous peoples. It was a familiar concept that the task of converting the unyielding adult pagans to Christianity would be a Herculean one; they therefore tended to turn their attention to children, whom they hoped to harness through the school system. Simply put, this was a strategy of 'catch them young'.

Given this strategy, the curriculum leaned heavily on three fundamentals – reading, writing and arithmetic, which were viewed to be sufficient to at least enable the educated converts to operate under the missionary banner, as interpreters, and the colonial administrative structure, as clerks.[14]

The missionary programme of educating the natives was consequently restricted initially to the limited objective of producing marginally literate Africans. It was envisaged that the products of this education would operate within their terrain and would therefore be able to transmit the new message of salvation to their own people, along with the ability to communicate with their European overlords. The main and perhaps the only concern of mission schools was to produce 'school masters', who would later become catechists, and then priests.

From the very beginning, the Christian missionary societies had a virtual monopoly on education. To all intents and purposes, the school was the church. The two institutions functioned simultaneously in a harmonious symphony. The church evangelist was also the village teacher. An appreciation of this fact is cardinal in considering the African educational system from its earliest stages.

From the standpoint of acculturation, the real significance of the missionary monopoly over education lay in the evangelical approach of mission schools. The mission schools were very powerful instruments for the rapid Christianisation and thus 'Europeanisation' of the youthful population. The schools taught young Nigerians to aspire to the virtues of Western Christian civilisation. They consciously encouraged the mutated European culture and indirectly fostered disdainful feelings towards their so-called heathen brothers.

Each Christian missionary outpost, be it Roman Catholic Mission (RCM), the CMS, etc., had a school running up to standard two; some were up to standard four. The central stations or parishes ran schools that conducted classes up to standard six, and produced the teaching workforce for the lower schools at the substations.

Data of CMS schools and locations in eastern Nigeria, 1921

	Onitsha	Owerri
Number of schools	173	206
Number of pupils	15,705	10,037
Number of teachers	344	289

From: Obi, C.A. (ed.), *A Hundred Years of the Catholic Church in Eastern Nigeria (1885–1985)*[15]

It has been shown that up to 1920, the missions took the lead in the drive towards establishing and expanding Western education in southern Nigeria, whether at primary, secondary or teachers' training levels. The role of the government from 1903 (in the colony and protectorate of southern Nigeria) had been to encourage the missions by offering guidelines and regulations, known as Education Codes, for the proper organisation and administration of the schools, as well as by granting financial subsidies. So long as those regulations did not negate the principal motive for which the missionaries founded the schools, there was no conflict with the government, especially in eastern Nigeria.

From the 1920s, however, Nigeria's colonial government started making serious moves for a more direct control of the school system. In 1922, an education consulting firm known as Phelps-Stokes was commissioned to undertake a detailed study of native education in tropical Africa and come up with recommendations. An advisory committee set up in 1923 based on the memoranda submitted by the commission published a comprehensive statement of imperial policy in the education sector. The committee report was published in 1925 in a white paper titled 'Education policy in British Tropical Africa'.[16]

The committee, in its report, touched on many aspects of education in British African colonies. But while it encouraged the existing cooperation between government and Christian organisations, it emphasised that the primary role of government was to "direct and supervise education delivery at the mission schools".

The report states that "Government welcomes and will encourage all voluntary educational efforts which conform to the general policy. But it reserves to itself the general direction of educational policy and the supervision of all educational institutions by inspection and other means."[17]

The above was the evolution of government's involvement in the education system, which culminated in the education code of 1926 that incorporated most of the recommendations of the advisory committee.

The code provided for, among other things, grants-in-aide for school buildings and teachers' salaries payable only to schools on the 'assisted' list. This type of partnership between colonial administration and Christian missionary societies proved to be a cheap way of training the youths who would be recruited into the growing civil and commercial service.

One of the major stipulations of the code was that academic pursuit in the mission schools would be limited to standard four, while students who were desirous of furthering their education could then transfer to Central Schools in order to progress up to standard six.

K.B.C. Onwubiko noted that each missionary substation had a school running up to standard two, a few others had up to standard four, and the central stations ran up to standard six with government assistance and produced teachers for the schools in the substations.[18]

After his baptism on 8 December 1918, Gabriel Nnolim and other converts were enrolled as the pioneer class of CMS elementary school under the tutelage of the first church teacher, Mr. Isaac Okonkwo, who hailed from Ufuma in the present Orumba south Local Government Area of Anambra State. He shared the same class as other 'early birds' like Thomas E. Umetiti, Reuben I. Egbunonu, Richard Okpala, Patrick Nwazo and David Umeasiegbu, among others. They were taught to read, write and calculate simple arithmetic, not forgetting Bible knowledge, which was at the crux of Western education. Strengthened by the successes recorded during elementary education, Gabriel (as he was now known) moved on to complete his standard-six primary education in 1925.

Chapter Three

Ready to Work in God's Vineyard

Successful completion of elementary standard four in 1923 was the needed launch pad for Gabriel to commence a life of service to God, the church and humanity.

As was the norm at that time and age, bright young school leavers were retained by their schools for temporal teaching jobs, or as pupils' instructors. Their job description included to help organise Sunday schools, guide pupils in sporting activities, and run errands for school teachers and church pastors.

Services rendered at this level were mostly appreciated but not remunerated, as the school leavers were seen as volunteers. They served as the intermediaries between the missionaries and the indigenous people, having become semi-literate and able to interpret the language of the white man to the locals and vice versa.

It was expected that these volunteers would remain in the services of their alma mater until they were able to further their education at the next level.

This was the lot of Gabriel between 1922 and 1923, when he served briefly as pupils' instructor, before he advanced to complete his standard six between 1924 and 1925. This short period of service in the school environment obviously gave Gabriel the necessary background for his later service to humanity; this was when Gabriel Nnolim cut his wisdom teeth in the art of developing other individuals through teaching Christian evangelism and community mobilisation.

With little support from the CMS in Umuchu, coupled with hard work and personal sacrifice, he was able to complete his standard six in 1925, at CMS Central School, Nkwere-Opiegbe in Orlu area that is now Imo State.

The central schools were also referred to as "Government Assisted Schools, because such educational facilities received some financial assistance by way of grants, unlike the elementary schools that were solely founded by most missions, where Pupils received education up to Form IV. Most boys, who passed Form IV, would do a two-year normal course in accordance with the education code".[19]

The Principal of Obosi Training Institution, Rev. J.E. Ibeneme, in his 1931 synod report on activities of the institution, described the life of students in the school thus:

"Some of the young men were very rough and careless at the start but God's Grace so did its noble work in them that before the end of the first six months they became changed men – very quiet, sober, careful and obedient. All worked heartily from the beginning to the end... One of the chief factors in the moulding of men's life and character here in our college is the Sunday service, held once or twice a month, at which Holy Communion is regularly administered and very careful exhortation given on God's Holy word. These services are occasions of our specially drawing near to the Lord and His drawing near to us."[20]

These activities ran in pari passu with out-of-class activities like games, scouting, social works, community service and itinerating etc.

A former bishop on the Niger, Rt. Rev. B. Lasbrey, had rationalised on the nexus between the church and the school, explaining that the schools were a very important part of the church's life. "A healthy church must be a literate church. Furthermore, our schools are great evangelistic agency. I think

I am right in saying that the large majority of those coming forward today for confirmation and Baptism are from the schools, and as in the past, so in the future, we shall, I believe be able to trace many of our outstanding workers as having been won to Christ while yet at school."[21]

Fascinated by his brief foray into teaching, Gabriel got the approval of the CMS mission in Ekwulobia Parish (from where the young church in Umuchu was administered) to go back to Obosi on scholarship. This time around, the purpose was clear and the focus was firm. His second trip to Obosi was specifically to enrol and complete his training as a teacher. His nomination by the mission station in Ekwulobia and subsequent approval for the scholarship programme by Onitsha Archdeaconry Education Board was based on his outstanding performance as a pupils' instructor at St. Thomas Primary School, Umuchu.

Thus, in 1929, Gabriel Nnolim successfully completed his teachers' training programme and became a certified church teacher and catechist from CMS Teacher Training institution located then within the precinct of St. Andrew's Church Ire-Obosi.

He acquired what could be described as 'double honours' as a Grade III teacher and third-class catechist from the teachers' higher elementary certificate examination he took in 1929. The examination was the entry-level qualification for church teachers in the CMS education system.

He was the first indigene of Umuchu to receive that level of education at the time.

Armed with this latest 'sophisticated' academic weaponry, Gabriel Nnolim Ezekwo began his more than fifty-year career in teaching and evangelism, which took him and his household to many communities in the former eastern Nigeria. In the cause of his career, he attended several refresher courses and trainings to sharpen his skills and improve his capacity. Based on this continuous learning process, he received promotions and reached the zenith of his calling (catechetics) and occupation (teaching).

His giant strides in the education system of the CMS of Nigeria, diocese on the Niger, are still visible, many years after his transition to the great beyond. He traversed the length and breadth of the old eastern Nigeria like a colossus, planting churches, evangelising people, establishing schools, teaching children, and gathering men and women for the development of their towns, as well as lighting up many rural communities with his torch of liberty, which is the freedom (from primordialism) that comes with education and enlightenment.

Having secured the basic requirement needed

to function as a church teacher and local church administrator, otherwise known as catechist, the young Gabriel Nnolim Ezekwo had become physically, emotionally and intellectually prepared to commence work in the vineyard of God.

By this time, the diocese on the Niger had expanded southwards into the interior parts of the southeast. With more mission stations, parishes and schools established in Owerri and Okigwe districts, there was increasing need for more human resources to be deployed into the services of the CMS.

The situation was made even worse following the death of many early missionaries and the retrenchment of most church workers from the West Indies. In 1932 alone, the Niger mission recorded the demise of seven highly valued workers in the Lord's vineyard, who were called for higher service into God's kingdom. The likes of Gabriel Ezekwo were readily available to fill the gaps and carry on with the work of Christian evangelism and propagation of Western-style literacy.

The diocesan education board met at the end of each year to evaluate issues concerning education administration, while a sub-committee on first appointments constituted under the synod also met at same time, when locations of first- and second-class catechists and evangelists (like Gabriel Ezekwo) from Obosi Training Institution were made to the various districts.[22]

Upon posting, these missionary light bearers were charged with the complicated task of evangelising, organising, educating and administrating the local mission stations as well as church groups within their areas of influence.

Rt. Rev. A.W. Howells, in 1932, rationalised that, "Some people there are who take objection to the work of Education as being distinct from Evangelistic work. Let us not forget that they are inseparable and the one is a nursery of the other. The missionary societies, particularly our own society, has today, what we know to schools and seminaries that have been run by different societies and we shall be ungrateful if we forget or break the bridge by which we have crossed over. Freely then we have received, let us freely give."[23]

Fired up with this charge, they marched through dangerous forest and bush paths. Armed with the torch of liberty that is elementary education and the Apostles' battleaxe, which is the Christian Bible, they traversed the entire Igbo hinterland with great zeal. Their commitment to succeed in this onerous task was insurmountable, just as their faith that God would lead them through the valleys and shadows of death remained unwavering.

Although they had a very minimal level of education when compared with pastors these days, those pioneers were very resolute, committed and convinced of their ecclesiastical vocation. They toiled day and night without much grease to their elbow. They worked selflessly without expecting any pat on the back. Their commitment to duty was unappreciated and unrewarded by the church hierarchy, yet their zeal and enthusiasm to take the gospel of Jesus Christ to the remotest parts of the land remains unrivalled even to date.

Notwithstanding their sophisticated level of studies in both theology and philosophy, it is believed most modern-day pastors and ministers begin their ministry with eyes fixated on pecuniary gains and wealth generation. This explains the drift by the clerical order from the theology of liberation and salvation to the misconceived theology of prosperity and riches of God's kingdom.

This screwed sense of the ministry of Jesus Christ on Earth has led astray many ministers in the temple of God. They become disillusioned and overwhelmed when they can't meet their mundane expectations.

In his days, however, ministers of God in the likes of Gabriel worked assiduously and selflessly. They were commissioned without remuneration; they worked out their salvation with the Bible as their only work tool; they travelled to all the nooks and crannies of our villages or communities without assisted means of transportation.

Some died of accidents and attacks on their way, like the late Jonathan Uchendu, a member of the tutorial staff of the teachers' training college in Awka, who met his untimely death in 1931 following a fatal accident. Then there was Rev. E.O. Ononye, an indigene of Onitsha, who was lost to the cold hands of death on 29 November 1931 at far-away Owerri district after a prolonged and poorly treated fever. On 31 December 1931, the Rev. J.O. Egbuche, also an indigene of Onitsha, had his ministry cut short at a remote village in Enugu, where he died of tuberculosis. The list is endless.

In spite of these challenges, those of them who had the benefit of long life such as Gabriel continued preaching the undiluted message of salvation for more than fifty years. This calls to mind the need for current church leaders to thoroughly examine the intentions of those aspiring to enlist as workers or pastors in the temple of God, in order to critically interrogate what drives them towards such aspiration, with a view to determine those truly propelled by the spirit of God, and those compelled by craze for wealth.

Such soul-searching background checks should

be done during the formative stages at various seminaries.

This proposition is in line with Christ's teaching on separating the wheat from the chaff, which will help check the current spate of endemic corruption and other vices that are believed to pervade among men of clerical collar in these days.

Chapter Four

Retracing His Giant Footprints

The need to retrace the path a giant has marched is to showcase his legacies, in order to serve as a signpost for future pathfinders. His legacies were as charismatic as his footprints were indelible, for "he went about doing good".

Like a colossus, he bestrode the landscape of old eastern Nigeria preaching the gospel to heathens and educating those that believed.

It took about two years of spine-breaking research to really retrace the footsteps and chronicle the legacies of Gabriel Ezekwo from the areas he served.

History is the attempt to discover the significant things about the past, on the basis of fragmentary evidence. It then follows that to recount the significant aspects of Gabriel's pastoral work, reliance must be made on fragments of documentary and oral evidences. Gabriel Ezekwo was among the first set of itinerant evangelists, also referred to as 'travelling teachers', appointed to roam about preaching the word of God, converting the pagan population of the hinterlands and tutoring them on how to read and write.[24]

Gabriel was posted to then Umuduru District in early 1930. The district constituted five groups, namely Umuduru, Anara, Okwelle, Amaraku and Ugiri.

The leadership of the CMS must have considered his previous experience in that area during his days as a student of the Higher Elementary School in Nkwerre-Orlu, before posting him back to that familiar terrain for him to begin his public service.

Upon being posted to Umuduru district, Gabriel commenced his fulfilled life of rural evangelism in Umunze-Umuduru in 1930.

In 1931, he was at St. John's Church, Osina, where he worked as both church worker and teacher at the CMS primary school, Osina. He was not mentioned in the church's centenary records though, largely because he was not officially stationed at the church but rather to the entire district, as an itinerant evangelist/teacher.

However, it was while working and living at Osina that he married his first wife, who later died in 1932 during childbirth.[25]

Pa Christian Ezekwo, an octogenarian who had lived with the missionary icon, recalled that Gabriel had told him stories of his missionary exploits in Osina, including the mobilisation towards the rebuilding of the CMS Primary School building, which was wrecked by a strong tornado. The wreckage, which led to a significant drop in the student population, was made worse following the inability of the few Christian converts to muster the required funds needed for the reconstruction work. Thus, this situation of despair needed the services of an astute fundraiser. Gabriel Ezekwo rose to the occasion and figured out a system of voluntary contribution by all adult men, regardless of their Christian denomination and religious inclination.

He subtly conscientised the local people on the need for them to make contributions towards the reconstruction. The charitable contribution was code-named 'UgwoOkporoJiakpu', meaning payment that every adult male should pay. As a result of this, the people willingly contributed their widow's mite towards the building of the new cement-block building for the CMS primary school.

The community donations he instituted continued until 1949, when the new school building was completed and commissioned. This block of classrooms existed until June 1999 when it was eventually pulled down to give way for a bigger building. He served the St. John's Christian community alongside Mr. Theophilus Moneme, who was the resident church worker/catechist.

After Osina, the evangelism-cum-education trailblazer was stationed at St. Silas Church Amucha, in Orlu area within the then Owerri district from 1933 to 1939. Over the years, the then Owerri district had grown to become an archdeaconry, then a diocese and now an archdiocese, with eleven sub-dioceses under it. Kudos to the selfless efforts of early foreign missionaries and indigenous evangelists, of which Gabriel Ezekwo was among the pioneers.

On 16 October 1935, Gabriel remarried and wedded Mercy Iloka from Umuomaku. At the time of their marriage, Mercy had just graduated from the famed St. Monica's Women's College at Ugwuoba.

The land and people of Amucha welcomed the Apostle of God as he was blessed with the birth of his first daughter in 1937. Comfort, as Gabriel named her, came to comfort the grieving soul of the evangelist, which was barely recovering from the agony of losing his first wife to the cold hand of death, during her first and only unsuccessful journey to motherhood.

Having worked hard to strengthen the Christian community at St. Silas Church Amucha, the evangelist later moved to Okazubike where he was stationed from 1940 to 1942. At Okazubike, the Lord's general was blessed with a second daughter. He named her Ozioma (meaning 'good news'). Obviously, this was meant to depict the mood of the evangelist who had dedicated his life to spreading the good news of the crucified Christ. The third daughter, Chinwe, also came in Okazubike.

The stallion of Christian evangelism then moved to Amaraku from 1943 to 1947. There he was blessed with the birth of a son, who he named Samuel, apparently in reminiscence of the divine call to service in God's vineyard that Prophet Samuel answered and dutifully carried out in 1 Samuel 3:10. Such a call to duty was what Gabriel committed his entire life to, serving God and humanity. Prior to Samuel, he was blessed with another daughter in Amaraku, named Chijioke. Many years later, Madam Mercy confided in their first son that the birth of four girls in quick succession attracted contemptuous comments from relations of her husband, who mocked and even suggested that Gabriel consider marrying another wife, as polygamy was one of the primordial practices of the people. But Gabriel's Christian beliefs would not allow such. Mama explained that she surmounted the intimidation with fervent prayers to God, like Hannah, the wife of Elkanah in 1 Samuel

1:20, "and she called his name Samuel, for she said, 'I have asked him of the Lord.'"

This prolonged wait before the coming of the first male child influenced Gabriel's emotional filial attachment with the young Samuel, as he could hardly beat the boy or physically punish him when he misbehaved. Samuel confessed to have taken advantage of his father's emotional attachment to commit several acts of indiscipline. Gabriel would rather choose to invite other teachers to punish Samuel for acts of infantile malady than to raise his own hand against the boy.[26]

There is a documented testimony of the crusaders' march on the soil of Anara Community, in present-day Ezihe Diocese. In the 1949 Report of Proceeding of the Third Session of the Sixth Synod for the Diocese on the Niger, the then venerable in charge of Umuduru District, in his report, appreciated Gabriel Ezekwo for working assiduously to raise money to pay the yearly assessment for all the churches under Anara group, except one or two which finished very late.[27]

This open commendation to Gabriel bore eloquent testimony and a confirmation that he was at Anara in 1948.

Thereafter, the flagship berthed at Amaimo in Ikeduru area, between 1949 and 1951. The resounding successes recorded thus far in his victorious missionary journeys must have informed his choice of the name Victor, which he gave to his third son who was born in Amaimo. Godson (meaning 'son of God'), his second son, had been born during their visit to Umuchu shortly before relocating to Amaimo.

St. John's Church in Obodo village, Amaimo played host to the household of Gabriel Ezekwo. An archival record of attendance to the meetings of the Women's Guild beginning from 1942, which was found in the possession of eighty-five-year-old retired teacher Pa Beniah Agwuka, clearly showed that Mrs. M.U. Ezekwo was the leader of the women's group between 1949 and 1951. The discovery of this archival document is without prejudice to the people's memory of the life and times Gabriel spent in the area. Pa Beniah Agwuka and eighty-six-year-old Sir Godwin Maduwuba still remembered the invaluable contributions of catechist Gabriel Ezekwo in the sustenance of CMS as well as the development of Amaimo in general.

Several requests for new parishes and for the creation of more districts was the natural consequence that followed the development and progress being manifested, both in structure and population of the CMS congregation, especially in southeastern Nigeria.

Based on popular demands, more districts were created in 1950 and more church stations were elevated to parish status.

The question of how to source competent hands to man these new creations confronted the leadership of the Anglican Church.

Having taken note of the enormous capabilities that some of the church workers like Gabriel had acquired over the years, it became pertinent to draft such outstanding evangelists from wherever they might be, in order to commence the task of nurturing the newly created parishes and districts. Like the holy book said, "Labourers are few but the harvest is plenty."

Gabriel Ezekwo was drafted from his former station in Amaimo to the new Ufuma district of the then Awka Archdeaconry. Holy Trinity Church Ufuma became the district headquarters for all the churches in the present Orumba North and South local government areas, including far-flung communities like Umunze, Owerre-Ezukala, Ndiowu, Ogbunka and Akpugoeze (in present Nkanu area Enugu state).

The evangelist par excellence first landed at St. James' Church Enuguabo-Ufuma in early 1952. As a teacher-cum-church-worker, he had cause to work in virtually all the churches and new parishes within the district, mobilising human and capital resources for God's work. At some point, he worked at the district headquarters, being Holy Trinity Church (Ufuma), St. Michael's and All Angels Church (Akpu), St. Mathias (Umuona) etc.

In appreciation for his sophistry in church administration, evangelical prowess and human relations acumen, the church of Nigeria in 1953 elevated Mr. Gabriel Nnolim Ezekwo to the rank of first-class catechist in the Awka archdeaconry of diocese on the Niger.

He was then posted to Immanuel Church Nawfija, where he resumed duties as resident catechist from 1954.

His long stay at Nawfija could be said to be during the most glorious and glamorous era of Anglicanism in that area. Ezekwo's nine years stewardship in the community has remained indelible in the minds of those he lived with. Tales of his legendary exploits have been transmitted from generation to generation, so much so that younger generations of people in that community who may not have interacted with Gabriel still tell stories of his extraordinary service in the town.

He had a daughter named Uche Edith Ezekwo (now Mrs. Odimegwu), who Gabriel fondly called 'Nawfija-Amaka'. This pet name epitomised his love for the land and people of Nawfija. According to eighty-one-year-old Pa Eric Nwagboso Onyeagba, he was the longest-serving catechist who successfully administered Immanuel Anglican Church, Nawfija for nine years without blemish.[28]

Gabriel and his household proceeded to Ezinifite in present Aguata Area in 1963 where he was the resident catechist in charge of Immanuel Anglican Church, Ezinifite until the outbreak of the Nigeria civil war in 1966. Available records show that Gabriel Ezekwo was the last catechist or unordained church worker who administered the church and prepared the ground for its elevation to the status of a district on 20 January 1968. Consequently, the first ordained vicar was posted to take charge of the church that has become the parish headquarters of the new Ezinifite district.[29]

Before and during the time of Gabriel Ezekwo's service in the area, Ezinifite was a church under Uga district. As such, it was pastors from St. James' Uga that visited intermittently to carry out weddings, baptism, Holy Communion and such other prerogatives of an ordained vicar, thereby leaving the day-to-day running of the church, community evangelism and management of schools in the able hands of the catechists.

Rev. J. Onyechi took over from Gabriel Ezekwo in 1967, following the elevation of the church to parish status. Like John the Baptist, Gabriel was a forerunner who prepared the ground or set the pace for the smooth take-off of the new parish.

From Ezinifite, Gabriel Ezekwo moved to St. Mark's Enugu-Agidi in late 1967 till late 1968. His stay at Enugu-Agidi was short and uneventful, largely because of the bloody civil war that was ongoing.

Samuel Ezekwo, who had graduated from Anglican Boys' Boarding Secondary School, Agulu, remembered coming home and meeting his father in a make-shift church, as the main church premises was taken over by soldiers as their military base.

As a result of continuous military combat operations in the area, church properties and records were totally destroyed. The church of God could be said to exist only in the hearts of men, as religious activities at St. Mark's Enugu-Agidi were practically at a standstill.

As a result, Gabriel was quickly redeployed to St. James' Church Uga by January of 1969, where he served until the end of the civil war in 1970. By this time, Col. Joe Achuzie and his troops used the church and the parsonage as a military camp. Gabriel relocated to the residence of Mr. Henry Nwosu of Umudim, Umu-Ekperechi in Awarasi village, Uga, who himself was also a member of the church parochial committee.

The Old St. James' Anglican Church, Uga

The proximity of the church to the Uga airstrip was probably one of the factors that informed the choice of the military in using it as a base.

Mrs. Basie Nneke (née Nwosu), the daughter of Mr. Henry Nwosu, whose family house provided shelter for the Ezekwos, affirmed that she remembered quite well the very hairy-bodied and dark-complexioned catechist who once lived in her father's compound when she was a little girl.

She insisted that her ability to still remember the catechist was as a result of the friendly disposition of the church administrator. According to Basie, the catechist was never deterred by the cataclysms of the war or the seizure of the church building because of the emergency situation of that time. Rather, he carried on his responsibilities enthusiastically, especially the task of distributing the food and relief materials brought in by foreign humanitarian organisations like the World Council of Churches (WCC).

With some clarity, she recalled how Samuel took his younger brother named Godson, in the company of other boys, including her elder brother, Dickson Nwosu, and courageously crossed the Rubicon by jumping into a steaming aeroplane that was about to take off after offloading its last freights at the Uga airstrip in January of 1970. The boys raced towards the cargo plane and jumped into it. The young Basie, alongside other children, mothers and fathers, watched in total bewilderment as their loved ones went away to an unknown destination, as Biafran refugees. Alas!! That was the last humanitarian cargo aircraft to depart the only remaining Biafra military enclave. Young Samuel had told his parents six months before the war ended that he would leave Biafra if they lost the war by any means, even if it meant hanging on the wheels of an aircraft. The parents did not believe him.

This audacious act, which was later to change the life and fortunes of the entire Gabriel Ezekwo household, is significantly similar to the courageous decision undertaken by the intrepid Gabriel Ezekwo some fifty-seven years earlier.

Perhaps it was in response to the genealogical urge to explore the opportunities of greener pastures in the city that prompted the young orphan to escape from the custody of his elder brother in 1913 with the intent to better his lot, by scaling through the mud fence of the family compound and undertaking a journey to Obosi.

In the face of obvious dangers, he meandered through bush paths by trekking for about twenty miles in search of the golden fleece. This journey must have taken several days, if not weeks, of sleeping and waking up in the forests, with all the attendant oddities and vagaries of living in a complete state of nature.

The decisive and heroic plunge into the world unknown was to be replicated in late January of 1970, when Samuel took his younger brother and a handful of other courageous young boys, jumped on board a cargo airplane. This audacious character of bravery and adventure seems like a trademark in the bloodline of the Ezekwos.

The plane took off to Gabon, a francophone West African country that supported the Biafran cause. When they landed in Gabon, the visibly malnourished and tattered-looking children of war-ravaged Eastern Nigeria were well catered for by their host government.

Back home, Pa Gabriel spent sleepless nights wondering what had become of his two children who had acquired the status of refugees in a strange land. Similarly, Madam Mercy was devastated by the unplanned departure of her boys to an unknown destination. They made supplications for God's guidance upon their kids. Gabriel's second daughter, Ms. Ozioma, who was already a registered nurse at that time, serving at the Red Cross Hospital in Awomama, recalled her several efforts to calm down their agitated parents, explaining to them that the boys would be fine. Going by her experience as an aide worker, she was sure that the boys were better off as refugees.

Gabriel Ezekwo and his remaining household spent the rest of 1970 in Uga rebuilding St. James' Church Uga after the damage caused by the military occupation of the church premises.

From Uga district, he was posted to Umuchu district, where he worked as catechist and teacher at St. Andrew's Anglican Church Ibughubu, in Umuchu, for three months beginning from January 1971.

St. Andrew's Ibughubu was under Umuchu district with a resident vicar at St. Thomas' Umuchu. Thus, apart from occasional visits by resident pastor Rev. A.O. Odilora, the entire work of church administration rested squarely on the catechist, Mr. Gabriel. Ezekwo.

At the cessation of hostilities, proposals were made for the creation of more districts in order to encourage the expansion of the Anglican Church. One such proposal, which received the prompt attention of the church hierarchy, was the proposal by Umuomaku groups.

The three church groups in Umuomaku were recognised and inaugurated as a district on 22 January 1970. It was carved out from the former Umuchu district under Awka archdeaconry.

An elaborate ceremony for the inauguration of the new district was graced by Rt. Rev. L.M. Uzodike, bishop on the Niger; the Rt. Rev. G.N. Otubelu, bishop of Enugu diocese; Ven. J.A. Onyemelukwe, the archdeacon Awka; Revs G.O. Abana, W.C. Ifemeludike, N.N. Anyiam and S.I. Umezinwa. As could be expected, these esteemed church leaders sought the services of the most experienced lay church administrator and possibly the oldest catchiest in Awka archdeaconry, Mr. G.N. Ezekwo.

The great servant of God arrived at St. Mary's

Anglican Church Umuomaku on 2 April 1971, and took over the administration of the young district from his predecessor and acting superintendent, Mr. C.C. Otubelu. The district consisted of church groups in Umuomaku, Agbudu and Onneh communities.

The three churches that make up the district did not have even one ordained vicar. As such, the catechist at St. Mary's had enormous responsibilities placed on his shoulders. Gabriel was not found wanting as he discharged these responsibilities creditably. This is evident in the comments made by bishops and pastors who visited Umuomaku during Gabriel's stewardship as contained in the visitors' notes and logbook of St. Mary's Church.

2/4/71

Arrived here with my family at about 6:30 pm.

G.N. Ezekwo, Ag Superintendent. Umuomaku District

3/7/71

Visited this church today and in a special service baptized twenty persons, admitted one person from RCM church and wedded twelve couples (12x2=24). It is marvelous in our eyes.

I thank God for giving the young District a dynamic worker of GN Ezekwo's caliber. The Acting

Superintendent here is undisputably dynamic, and the flock responds correspondingly.

AO Odilora
Pastor & Superintendent Umuchu

21/9/71

I visited this morning for annual confirmation service and took confirmation for 25 candidates. There were also 27 candidates admitted to the Diocesan women's Guild. I am highly impressed with the satisfactory progress noticed in the work of the District. I hope that other churches in the District are as alive to their future as the mother church St. Mary's.

I am very much delighted with the co-operation among the staff of the school and the church. May the Lord bless the work here and bless the workers and also his children who serve him daily in His Church.

L.M. Uzodike Bp

This dynamic, astute and committed labourer in the Lord's vineyard was so much appreciated by the Anglican Church that in 1972 he was made acting superintendent of Umuomaku District, a position that was supposed to be held by ordained priests. He was consequently invited to and represented his district at the Synod of Diocese on the Niger, held at Christ Church Onitsha from 28 to 31 May 1972.

families. He came back to the Parsonage at 2:55pm and began the evening service during which 26 infants were baptized. It was a very busy day for us all.

I thank the Umuomaku and their Catechist for their wonderful hospitality given me in the name of the Lord. May God bless their work. Amen.

A.O. Oji***
Pastor & Supdt. Umuohia

2/4/71 · Arrived here with my family at about 6:30 p.m.

L.M. Ezekwo.
Ag. Superintendent
Umuomaku district.

3/7/71 Visited this Church today, and in a special service baptized twenty persons, admitted one person from R.C.M. Church, and wedded twelve couples (12×2 = 24). It is marvellous in our eyes.

I thank God for giving this young District a dynamic worker of L.N. Ezekwo's calibre. The Acting Superintendent here is undisputably dynamic and the flock responds correspondingly.

A.O. Oji***
Pastor & Supdt. Umuaha.

21/9/71 I visited this morning for the Annual Confirmation Service and took Confirmation for 25 candidates.

These were also 27 candidates admitted to the Diocesan Women Guild. I am highly impressed with the satisfactory progress noticed in the work of the District. I hope that other Churches in the District are as alive to their future as the Mother Church St. Mary's.

I am very much delighted with the Cooperation among the staff of the School & the Church.

May the Lord bless the work here and bless the workers and also His Children who serve Him daily in His Church.

I am grateful for the warm reception that was given me by the staff & members.

L.H.Chodike ***

The visitors' notes and logbook of
St. Mary's Church, Umuomaku

The renowned catechist continued to work in God's vineyard despite his old age until 1974 when he officially retired from active service, having served the Anglican Communion for a record-breaking fifty-one years.

Ide Gabriel Ezekwo's original stone country home, 1943

Even in retirement he continued to take part in church activities, attending church synod meetings, preaching at various churches, mentoring young clergies and promoting Anglican evangelism wherever he found himself.

The new stone country home of Ide Gabriel Ezekwo

Mr Eleazer Umeanulugwo showing the old
parsonage built by Gabriel Ezekwo

St. Mary's Parish, Umuomaku

Monument erected in memory of past catechists
in St. Mary's Church, Umuomaku

Mr. Evans Anyawu showing the investigator the
ruins of former St. John's Primary School

1949 register of members and attendance of Women's Guild
meeting, showing Mrs. M.U. Ezekwo as the leader

(L-R) Ejiofo Umegbogu, Joel Onyeagba, Samuel Ezekwo
and Kingsley Onyeagba

The dilapidated Catechist (Ide) Gabriel N. Ezekwo
Memorial Chapel and Umuchu Unity Center, (aka
St. Thomas Stone Church) before renovation

Chapter Five

Harvest of Legacies

As the saying goes, "a journey of a thousand miles begins with a single step". That was exactly how Pa Gabriel's fifty-one-year journey of a life of service to God and to humanity started, with that bold attempt to escape from the guardianship of his elder brother, Ezeonyirimba, and undertake a perilous journey to Obosi. That audacious trip to a strange land really opened the eyes of the young Nnolim to the vista of opportunities that abound in acquiring Western education and working for God.

Gabriel blazed the trail, when he scaled the fence in his father's compound against all odds and trekked more than twenty miles through those jungle tracks, to and from Obosi, in 1913 to embrace Christianity and Western education. The odds were many and varied. Those were the days of active slave trade in

West Africa, when slave raiders used to waylay travellers and capture young men and women for shipment to plantations in America and the West Indies. He was quoted as saying that he had to be very careful as he trekked, praying and watching his movements carefully so that he would not be captured by the slave raiders who lurked around on the traveller's path. He also said that God protected him during this journey, by revealing potential dangers leading him to change travel paths. It meant that he had to trek for more days and longer distances.

It may be argued that this dangerous trip was an unsuccessful outing, because it was cut short by obvious lack of finance and/or sponsorship. But the exposure garnered during this period propelled him to immediately grab the opportunity of Christian baptism and Western education, as soon as the opportunity offered itself, in 1916 when CMS was brought to Umuchu through the instrumentality of other indigenous Christian pioneers like Emenike Orachusi and Chief Ezeanyim Ezenwaka.

Unlike other pioneers, he had seen and tested the civilising influence of the white man, and so was more favourably disposed to embrace 'new ways'.

His interaction with the first Igbo clergy, the Rev. George Nicholas Anyaebunam, and other missionary pioneers during this time, positively influenced his life of service to God. The young Gabriel was able to navigate his way through primary education despite his poor and humble background, as he had to combine his classroom work with other acts of peasantry to make ends meet.

By the time he finished his early education and returned to Obosi, then as a teacher-trainee, Gabriel was already a mature young man, filled with so much energy and vitality to succeed. Among his peers, he was well known for his love of physical drills, sporting activities and the English language (he was nicknamed the grammarian). He always maintained that such physical exercises helped to improve strength, fitness and stamina, which are needed for the energy-sapping task of rural-rugged evangelism.

This explains why his physical outlook was striking in his youth and into his old age. He was smooth faced, and his fresh skin, hairy body and well-developed figure bespoke a man in good physical condition through active exercise, yet well content with mundane fortunes.[30]

Upon completion of his training at the teachers' training college, Obosi, Gabriel had an avalanche of opportunities to secure employment in the fast-growing mercantile outlets or public service establishments at the cities of Onitsha, Lagos,

Kaduna etc. These job opportunities offered better remuneration and welfare packages for the few literate indigenous people, yet Gabriel continued to experience an irresistible inner call from God to serve Him and humanity through evangelism. Like the biblical Samuel and other prophets and apostles of God, he answered the divine call. A call to serve, not on the supposedly more beneficial British colonial civil service or business establishments, but to serve in God's vineyard and contribute significantly in the salvation ministry of Christ by drawing many men and women to God.

Thus, Gabriel commenced a fifty-one-year odyssey to propagate Christ's message of eternal life for those that believed in Christ the Messiah, specifically among the Igbo people of eastern Nigeria. Like a stallion, he bestrode the eastern heartland with only one mission…to draw more men to God so that they may be reconciled with their creator through Christ, whose blood was shed on the cross of Calvary for the atonement of mankind.

At this time, Gabriel held sway as the first indigene of Umuchu to have attained that level of education. While his contemporaries at St. Thomas' CMS Primary School either dropped out or diverted into other fields of endeavour, Gabriel Ezekwo remained resolute in his search for the golden fleece.

His effort climaxed with his qualification as a teacher and church worker (lay evangelist).

Recall that he had tested his hands in the art of teaching when he volunteered his services as a pupils' instructor, shortly before enrolling for higher elementary school. Most certainly, this was when he got attracted to the noble profession of teaching.

Armed with his teacher's certificate, Gabriel accepted his posting to the then Owerri Archdeaconry. Specifically, to Umuduru district. This was where Gabriel spent many of his youthful years planting new churches, strengthening existing Christian groups, establishing schools, and mobilising and converting heathen people into followers of Christ, otherwise referred to as 'Christians'.

From a church worker, he grew through the ladder to become a first-class catechist, and finally, district superintendent. From grade III teacher, he rose through the ranks to become a headmaster to many schools.

Christian Evangelism

Regrettably, there is a dearth of information about Gabriel's missionary journeys due to a lopsided pattern of maintaining church records within the Anglican Communion skewed against lay church workers in favour of ordained clergy. Many church records are stored in the memory of the congregation and even when attempts were made to document them, only the activities of a few pastors and bishops were recorded. This lopsided system of documenting church history leaves out the monumental achievements of other categories of non-ordained torchbearers, who in fact were the fulcrum of the early church. Anglican faithful live and die with this memory, which lives in posterity with little or no record of the toils and sweats of our local church administrators and lay evangelists.

At the slightest prompting, this missionary extraordinaire could recount off-hand about thirty Anglican churches he established or helped to sustain in communities around old Owerri and Niger dioceses. But the documented history of most of these churches started and ended with a tribute to the clerical order, with little or no mention of lay workers. This accentuates the age-long saying that history does not remember soldiers who fought in the battlefields, but kings who ruled in the palaces.

One of Gabriel's earliest giant strides was after his graduation from the teachers' training college when he was posted to resume duties as a church teacher at then Owerri Archdeaconry in 1930. As an itinerant evangelist, his job was to convert people to the 'new way', and teach them Bible knowledge, as well as how to read and write, then ensure that they were baptised into CMS church and nurture them till they received the Holy Communion. He was quite aware that this schedule of responsibilities would certainly take him away from his people for a long time to come. But ideas, they say, rule the world, and men of ideas surely have a place in the history of mankind.

Gabriel conceived an idea that would help bring together the new crop of young Anglican converts who had cause to migrate to other towns either in search of the golden fleece or greener pastures in the growing city centres and the home-based Christian converts. Thus he founded an organisation called St. Thomas Church General Meeting Home and Abroad Membership. This organisation offered membership to Christian converts residing in Umuchu and those in diaspora. He envisioned that bringing together the Umuchu Christians who were living at home and those living abroad through this organisation would encourage think-home mentality and spur growth of the church and town development.

It was very difficult for him to source members of the church who were living abroad at that time and get them to interact with other Christian brethren living at home. This became even more problematic considering that the man at the centre of this earliest effort to invent a mechanism for social interaction was working at far-away Owerri-Okigwe area. With little means of communication and transportation, it was indeed a herculean task connecting other sons and daughters of Umuchu living elsewhere. Such was the burden of leadership that providence entrusted on the young Gabriel in his position as the most learned person from Umuchu at that time, having acquired the highest level of education over and above all his contemporaries. It was a leadership responsibility he did not shy away from, but saw as a challenge, which by the grace of God would be surmounted.

Nevertheless, as it is usually said that "where there is a will there must be a way", he persevered. He defied the dangers of long and tortuous journeys from his place of work to his hometown, consulted and convinced Anglican adherents to join the new church-based organisation. The goal of this foremost organisation was to engineer a system that would engender cross-fertilisation of ideas for better socio-religious interaction with the objectives of building a kind of homogeneity that would bring development and progress in any human society.

St. Thomas' General Meeting (Home and Abroad) founded in 1930, initially for only male members, was later expanded to include female members of the

Anglican Communion in Umuchu. Gabriel Ezekwo became the first chairman and later became the life patron of the organisation.

This group still exists to date and functions as a community-based organisation with countless achievements and visible projects executed in the church, in particular, and the town as a whole.

Despite his strenuous work schedule as a roving teacher and missionary, he had more lofty ideas on how to impact positively on the life of his people at home.

Deploying the experiences garnered during the formation of the aforementioned group, Gabriel took it a step further to establish UIU in 1937, as an administrative structure that comprised all segments of the community. As a constituent assembly of all citizens, the UIU consisted of pagan and Christian elements, regardless of denomination, education, gender or social status. Gabriel was able to bring together at this forum all the segments of the community, which existed as a set of fragmented villages living as republican units and administered independently by elders, who were selected in a gerontocratic-style democracy.

Standing on the pedestal of these two groups, Gabriel Nnolim Ezekwo triggered a series of actions that led to a boom in Christian evangelism and

Western enlightenment in the hitherto traditional society.

Remarkably, Gabriel used the church-based organisation as the microcosm, and the community-based institution as the macrocosm, for the mass movement that commenced and completed the monumental construction of St. Thomas' stone church project.

By this system of community mobilisation, Gabriel ensured that believers (of all denominations) and non-believers alike contributed in one way or the other to the building of St. Thomas' Anglican Church. The people virtually dropped their entire sectarian or parochial interests to regularly come out en masse to quarry stones and carry them on their heads, trekking long distances, mostly bare-footed, to supply at the construction site. Those living abroad sent in their meagre resources to ensure the smooth completion of the project.[31]

The iconic stone church was officially opened in 1955 as a regular place of worship for the Anglican denomination. It was one of the best of its kind in the Niger diocese in those days and accommodated worshippers from far-away Achina, Umuomaku, Enugu-Umuonyia etc.[32]

The massive stone structure is very significant to the entire good people of Umuchu, whose forebears contributed to its construction. It occupied a special place in the heart of Pa Gabriel throughout his lifetime. This explained why he inspired and encouraged the construction of another church building upon his return to the community in January 1975, seeing that this dear stone church had become overcrowded, and the facilities overstretched.[33] But he insisted that the new project should be done separately, without restructuring or demolishing the stone architecture.

The modern church project, which was started in September 1984 (during Gabriel's lifetime), has since been completed, dedicated and elevated in 2006 to the status of an archdeaconry in Aguata diocese.

Speaking of Gabriel Ezekwo's contributions to the growth of Christianity in Umuchu, Venerable David Obiagboso described him as "an institution in Christianity, because he changed the landscape of this town and convinced the people of this area that there is a supreme being. He was not the only missionary from this community, but he embraced Christianity and took it to the widest imagination. You cannot talk about Christianity here without talking about Gabriel Ezekwo. He soaked himself in Christianity. He travelled out to learn many things that Christianity brought to other towns, brought back those wonderful ideas and convinced his people on why they must follow the new way."[34]

His passion for God's work and doggedness in rural evangelism coupled with his natural gift of excellent human relations often garnished with a good sense of humor, enabled him to record quite a number of achievements in all the communities he lived and worked in. Among his greatest legacies to the Anglican Church in Nigeria were the stone churches that he mobilised the people to build in most of the areas in which he served. Several of these stone churches have been demolished, but the ones still standing remain landmarks in those communities to date.

The small Christian groups he organised in those years, consisting of few converts, have spread in leaps and bounds to become large Christian communities today, while the small church halls he built have now given way for gigantic church buildings. St. John's Anglican Church Osina celebrated its centenary in December 2016, with four additional churches created out of the mother parish. They include Church of Christ Osina, Church of New Bethel Osina, All Saints' Church Uzii, and Church of Divine Grace Umualaoma, all established to the growth of the present Osina archdeaconry.

Due to the growth of the Anglican community

in Osina and the viability of the church, because of the solid foundation laid by Gabriel and his contemporaries, the bishop of Ideato diocese, Rt. Rev. G.C. Echefu, elevated Osina Christian community to the status of archdeaconry, with St. John's as the archdeaconry headquarters. The school where Gabriel taught has been expanded into a seminary school, now known as St. John Chrysostom Seminary.

St. John's Parish now has a bigger church building, but the model stone church that Gabriel facilitated still stands. This was the only stone-built church in the then Ndizuogu district. The quality of the stone used in erecting the church speaks volumes about the zeal and spirit of the local people. They carried those stones on their heads with great enthusiasm from a quarry called 'Ugwu Onuzoiyi' to the church building site.

Also in Amaraku, the Lord's servant found a mud church building with a thatched roof called St. Ebenezer's Church, built in an expanse of land donated by Chief Nnorum Njoku. Ab initio, St. Ebenezer's CMS Church was situated at the courtyard of the Mbamara royal family of Amaraku kingdom. This ancient kingdom was divided into three autonomous communities by Imo state government, for the sake of administrative convenience and ease of development.

Site of school where Pa Gabriel taught, now a seminary

On arrival, catechist Gabriel Ezekwo in his usual strategy commenced the building of a befitting house of worship for God. In a manner that was unprecedented in the history of the community, he ingeniously galvanised human and material resources from both Christians and heathens alike, to start a massive church project.

He got the then bishop of Niger diocese, the Rt. Rev. Cecil Patterson, to come to Amaraku on 31 August 1946 for the foundation-laying ceremony of the new church. St. Ebenezer's Church was subsequently renamed St. Peter's Anglican Church by Rt. Rev. Patterson, as proposed by the resident catechist, Gabriel Ezekwo. The church project was subsequently completed and dedicated to the glory of God on 20 December 1956, by Rt. Rev. S.M. Nkemena under Rev. S.C. Agulefo as superintendent of Umuduru district.

Eighty-eight-year-old Chief Fredrick Nnanna Nnorum (alias Eziokwubundu of Amaraku-Amaise), the son of the late benefactor of St. Peter's Church, Mr. Nnorum Njoku, testified to the fact that Gabriel was an extraordinary evangelist who went from house to house, visiting people, attending to their personal needs, preaching the gospel of Christ to the heathens and converting many to Christianity.

Despite the insuperable difficulties of discharging missionary responsibilities at that time without requisite logistics and communication aides, Gabriel bore true witness to the salvific ministry of Christ on Earth by passionately preaching the gospel of hope, salvation, and redemption wherever he went. Amaraku people benefitted immensely from the untiring efforts of this exceptionally selfless evangelist to expand the frontiers of God's kingdom. Today, the foundation that Gabriel laid has blossomed into an archdeaconry with capacity to host the synod of Okigwe North diocese in 1995. It has even moved on to beget two other big churches, namely St. Andrew's Church Umueli-Amaraku and Church of Holy Spirit at Umuobasi-Amaraku.

He repeated this feat at Immanuel Anglican Church Ezinifite, in Aguata Local Government Area of Anambra State. During his four-year stewardship, the church grew in both membership and financial base leading to its successful elevation to the status of a parish in 1968. On assumption of duty at Ezinifite, Pa Gabriel Ezekwo found a mud house, which served as the parsonage. He immediately mobilised resources and convinced church members of the need to build a more solid house as a place of residence for the catechist. He started the project and successfully completed it. However, he couldn't live in the house because he was transferred almost immediately after completing the project.

Fortunately enough, that house became a place of residence for the first pastor, who took over the administration of the church from Gabriel, when Immanuel Anglican Church became a parish.

According to Mr. Eleazer Umeanulugwo, who was then the president of the Boy's Brigade in the church, Gabriel frequently went on home visitations to pray for the sick, preach to the youths, and play with kids. "He loved to play with children a lot. That time he had a Baboon called 'Jatoh', which he kept in front of his house to attract children."

In that way, the great fisher of men lured many young people to church activities and enrolled them into CMS central school, which was under the supervision of this dynamic catechist.

The unflinching commitment and passion of this great apostle of Christ to see that Christianity was entrenched in Igbo land are still being eulogised in Nawfija community, Orumba South Local Government Area even half a century after his sojourn to that area.

As former Regent of Nawfija and chairman of the Elders Council of the community, Chief Eric Onyeagba recounted how the Anglican faithful were without a church building and they used the CMS Primary School (now community primary school) as a makeshift church until catechist Gabriel Ezekwo came to the town. He explained that the catechist, in consort with the then paramount ruler, Chief Joel Okoli, helped acquire the current expanse of land where Immanuel Anglican Church was built.

Then, the enormous task of building a gargantuan place of worship for the Anglican community in the town commenced in earnest.

Gabriel Ezekwo, in his characteristic manner, deployed his talent, time and energy to traverse the entire community and managed to galvanise human and material resources for the building of a befitting place of worship for the Anglican mission.

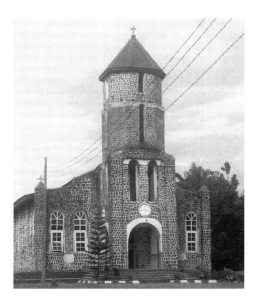
Immanuel Anglican Church Nawfija

When the then bishop on the Niger, Rt. Rev. C.J. Patterson, received stories of the positive impact that Gabriel was making in Nawfija, the cleric dispatched his assistant, Rt. Rev. S.M. Nkemena, to the small community. On 9 December 1958, the foundation stone-laying ceremony was conducted by no less a person than the first Igbo Anglican bishop, Rt. Rev. Samuel Nkemena. The building project continued with such a great speed until Pa Gabriel Ezekwo left the community in 1963.

It was eventually completed in 1990 and dedicated on 1 April 1991 by his lordship the Rt. Rev. M.S.C. Anikwenwa.[35]

Today, a giant stone church building stands in Nawfija community as another signature project of catechist Gabriel Ezekwo.

The leadership of Awka archdeaconry could no longer accept appeals from the Anglican community in Nawfija asking that catechist Gabriel be retained there, having granted several such requests in the past, which led to the long period that the servant of God had to spend among the people.

Within the nine-year period that he bestrode the landscape of the community, the Anglican congregation increased tremendously in membership. Gabriel was noted to have won more souls for God and converted a great number of heathens into Anglicanism, so much so that two new churches were established during his time, namely St. Mark's Anglican Church Umu-Owaya village and St. Peter's in Umu-Ezeogbu, both in Nawfija.

It was also during this period that the uncommon missionary gathered a small group of converts in an isolated community called Umuona. This group later metamorphosed into a huge Anglican congregation known presently as St. Matthias Church, Umuona.

His notable contributions towards the propagation of the gospel brought unprecedented growth to the Anglican Church in the area, to the extent that Nawfija was elevated to the status of a parish and inaugurated as a district headquarters with St. Mark's and St. Peter's as affiliates, shortly after the uncommon missionary left for Ezinifite in present Aguata Local Government Area.

It is needless to restate the fact that he achieved a strikingly similar feat at Immanuel Church Ezinifite, where his dexterity in rural evangelism and administration of local churches led to the elevation of the church to parish status in 1966. It was scheduled to be officially pronounced in a ceremony in 1967, but was later held on 20 January 1968, due to some administrative delays. This took place under Rev. J.A. Onyechi, who took over a booming and flourishing church from the last catechist to be in charge of the church – Mr. G.N. Ezekwo. This elevation to a district status was made manifest following the construction of a place of residence for the clergy, known as a parsonage, which Pa Gabriel Ezekwo commenced and completed during his stay.

Mr. Eleazer Umeanulugo recounted that, "When he came here, he met a mud house, which serves as the parsonage or residence of catechists. He immediately mobilised resources and convinced church members on the need to build a solid house with cement blocks and zinc, as a place of residence called vicarage befitting for a resident priest/vicar. He started the building project and completed it successfully. However, he couldn't live in that house because he was transferred almost immediately after completing the project. But that landmark achievement helped us to fulfil a necessary condition for the elevation of the church to a parish status, with a resident priest."[36]

What other ways could one evaluate and better appreciate the invaluable contributions of this uncommon missionary to Anglican evangelism in eastern Nigeria than to glance through a seventy-year-old visitors' logbook of St. Mary's Church Umuomaku, to see the heartfelt commendations passed by notable clerics who also worked in God's vineyard during the time of Gabriel Ezekwo, as the catechist superintending the affairs of the church in the area.

The church, which started in 1919, had existed as a mission group under Agulu, Ekwulobia and Umuchu districts at different times. On 22 January 1970 it was inaugurated as a district by bishop on the Niger Rt. Rev. L.M. Uzodike, assisted by bishop of Enugu diocese, Rt. Rev. G.N. Otubelu, archdeacon of Awka, Ven. J.A. Onyemelukwe and a host of other clergy.

This was made possible through the efforts of refugee pastors who lived and worked in the area as a result of the negative impact of the civil war in their own churches. It was the war-time policy of the Anglican community in Nigeria that any pastor or worker who moved away from his church or district as a result of war-time disturbances must find any church in the undisturbed areas in which to do God's work.

So Rev. G.A. Iloaba from St. Mary's Obosi, and the archdeacon of Enugu, Ven. H.I. Okechukwu, came to live in Umuchu district and served in St. Mary's Umuomaku, which was a tributary of St. Thomas' Anglican Church Umuchu district. These men of God brought their experience to bear, culminating in the inauguration of St. Mary's as a district.

Having inaugurated the young district, the church hierarchy was mindful of the fact that the young district needed the touch of an experienced administrator and soldier of Christ to pilot its affairs, following the departure of the refugee pastor at the end of hostilities. These qualities they found in abundance in catechist Gabriel Ezekwo. Gabriel was immediately dispatched to the area to midwife the nascent district.

On 3 August 1971, an equally remarkable servant of God, Rev. A.O. Odilora, visited Umuomaku Church and logged off with the following words of appreciation: "I thank God for giving this young district a dynamic worker of G. N. Ezekwo's calibre.

The Acting Superintendent here is undisputedly dynamic, and the flock responds correspondingly."

This was an open commendation in appreciation of the dynamism observed in the manner in which the uncommon evangelist commenced active service in Umuomaku, increasing the flock of Christ through conversion, baptism and matrimony, within just two months of assuming duties.

Even ordained pastors and renowned clerics marvelled at the electrifying enthusiasm with which Gabriel engaged the local populace in God's work.

With such scintillating vivacity, Gabriel, in his trademark, stimulated the interest of people to freely donate their time, energy and resources towards the building of a proper place of worship for God.

On 28 March 1972, barely one year to his retirement from active service, Gabriel laid the foundation stone for a bigger church structure with the support of the people and prayers offered to God Almighty for the successful completion of the project. The church was later completed and dedicated to God by Bishop Maxwell Anikwenwa.

In a meeting of the appointments board of the diocese on the Niger held on 25 October 1972 at Christ Church Onitsha, the chairman of the board and bishop on the Niger, Rt. Rev. L.M. Uzodike, announced the retirement of catechist G.N. Ezekwo, with effect from December 1973. The announcement came with a proviso that the Bishop reserved the discretionary powers to alter the retirement date "if the situation warranted it."[37]

Thus, it pleased his Lordship to extend Gabriel's retirement from service for another year. The bishop's motive may not have been unconnected with the need to allow the aged catechist some more time to raise the ongoing church building to a reasonable extent before exiting from God's work.

By 29 December 1973, when Gabriel was billed to bow out of service, he was still in a high spirit, winning more souls to God and bringing multitudes to worship Christ in His alter of grace with infectious enthusiasm – so much so that the visiting pastor and superintendent of Umuchu passed the following verdict on his stewardship in the young district.

I visited this church and worshipped, during which fifteen children were baptized, 103 men received Holy Communion. After the service, I wedded Mr. and Mrs. Innocent Onwuka in a colorful service attended by a large crowd. It was extremely grand.

I am greatly impressed at the progress of this young District. Their cheerfulness and large attendance are always sources of Joy to me whenever I come here.

I pray that God may strengthen them and help them to complete their new church building as early as possible. I am grateful to the Acting superintendent Mr. G.N. Ezekwo and his committee for their kind hospitality to me.

A.O Odilora
Pastor Umuchu

With near certainty, any discernible mind could conclude, it was this excellent scorecard that led the bishop to exercise his discretionary powers and retain Gabriel in the service of the diocese for one more year. With this type of report, the church couldn't get enough of this great servant of God. But like the Ecclesiastes said, "there is time for everything", a time to work and a time to rest. Whenever this universal law is contravened, nature will certainly show proof of his supremacy over mortals.

Thus, when the archdeacon of Awka, Ven. P.O. Egolum, visited on 2 July 1974, to introduce the new superintendent of Umuchu district, in the person of Rev. L. Ezeani, the visitor met the aged catechist who was struggling to recover from a protracted illness. Although they thanked God for the rare gift of a catechist in the calibre of Gabriel, they prayed for his recovery and wished him good rest. They were, however, quick to observe that the work of the church building was progressing very slowly and called for the work to be hurried along.

Obviously, the spirit was very willing but the body had become increasingly weak.

But suffice it to say that his alluring personality enabled him to easily endear himself to the hearts of people wherever he went. His strong conviction to win souls for God was strongly driven, so much so that he would deny himself all sorts of personal comfort, family consort and the opportunities to acquire material wealth, only to see that the salvific ministry of Christ spread to all the nooks and crannies of Igbo land.

As a church worker-cum-evangelist with little education and remuneration, he won more souls to God in very remote communities where better educated and paid pastors fear to tread. With his strong character and personal conviction he did not hesitate to take action with boldness, so enthusiastically that his host communities could not but join him in worshiping the Almighty God, whose grace was the ultimate source of his audacious hope to succeed, even in the face of glaring poverty and sufferings.

And the supreme architect of the universe did not hesitate to momentarily bless his efforts with new converts who trooped to his churches. Like a colossus, Gabriel did not hesitate to take advantage of this opportunity to stamp his feet on the sands of time by not only making a direct impact on the lives of the people, but to also ensure that he left monumental legacies by building houses of worship for God's children.

Evidently, the churches he established immediately became a veritable nest of salvation for all God's children who fell into the dragnet of this great fisher of men. Those who believed and were baptised became partners in the ultimate redemptive sacrifice for the atonement of sins, which Jesus Christ performed at the cross of Calvary.

Fired up by the spirit of Pentecost imbibed via the scriptural teachings of this exceptional catechist, the congregation in unison, like a colony of bees, commenced a series of activities that would eventually culminate in a flourishing body of Christ.

Community Development

Gabriel was creative enough to always consider new ways of doing things and new ways of reaching his target audience to minister the undiluted word of God. This was a duty that he believed he owed society. And he discharged this duty with one focus: fellowship with God through service to humanity.

He believed firmly that the church cannot exist in isolation but must grow in peace with the populace it serves. His disposition was always that the congregation is part of the community. As a community leader par excellence, Gabriel developed a system of strategic collaboration between the Christian elements and the pagan population of any community where his ship of Christian evangelisation berthed.

In his days, many communities did not easily accept Christianity because of the competing interests in their cultural practices and other primordial sentiments. The wrongly perceived disruptive tendencies of the new religion and the accompanying Western enlightenment brought about constant conflict between churches and communities. To resolve such an apparent clash of two cultures, Gabriel Ezekwo conceptualised and to a large extent practicalised a relationship model that worked. This model allowed him to plant new churches, expand existing Christian groups and, at the same time, work with the local populace to ensure the provision of amenities/infrastructure that enhanced the living standard of the entire community.

His amiable character and sense of humour allowed him to easily cultivate good rapport with the local populace.

Typically, he organised town union meetings or community development associations comprising local leaders who worked with the churches to resolve conflicts among people or between Christian denominations.

He used town unions to canvas for school pupils and in many cases offered scholarships to indigent ones. He was able to institute education scholarship schemes and development funds in most areas he served. Through this means, a lot of young people who could not afford Western education were given opportunities to further their academic pursuit, thereby increasing the human development index of those areas that came under his influence.

As the saying goes, "charity begins at home". Gabriel had experimented on this model in his hometown when he founded the UIU in 1937.

Basking in the euphoria of the successes achieved in establishing the first socio-religious group in Umuchu comprising of men and women of Anglican denomination, and banking on the enormous confidence reposed on him as the most educated man in the town at that material time, Gabriel Ezekwo worked tirelessly to put in place a socio-political organisation, comprising Christians (from every denomination) and heathens alike. His main objective was for his community to have a non-discriminatory, non-religious and all-encompassing administrative structure, which would enable the gerontocratic society to fit into the emerging world order.

Criss-crossing the narrow and dangerous routes between Owerri area (in present Imo state), where he was designated for missionary service, and Umuchu (in Anambra State), where he hailed from, Gabriel had a daunting task travelling home to convince his kinsmen of the need to come together regardless of creed or belief, to form an organisation that could provide leadership for the seemingly disjointed communities that were only brought together during cultural festivals.

Before this time the only available structure for the cross-pollination of ideas was through the meetings of the fourteen age grades. He then united these age grades and merged them with the Christian groups existing then to form a single super-structure.

Prior to the formation of this union, Gabriel had, in 1930, experimented with the idea of forming an administrative structure that would hold the people together in a symphony of brotherhood. He led other youths of the community to clear the Okpete (sugarcane) bush situated between Uchu shrine and the Salvation Army Church. That was where the 'Odo-Okpoto' meeting started, which included elders, chiefs and leaders of age grades. Considering the patriarchal nature of the society in the immediate pre-colonial era, it was easy for the elders to hijack and turn the meeting into a quasi-customary court gathering where inter-personal and inter-village disputes were adjudicated. More so, these elders were said to have perverted justice because of their clannish and selfish interests, which was contrary to the aim of setting up the group.

This uncharitable situation continued until December of 1937, when Gabriel came home and assembled other like minds, including Benson Emenike, William Ojiakor, Charles Unigwe, Jonah Ezekwo, Michael Metu, Jonathan Ojiako and Jeremiah Otti among others, and established the Umuchu Improvement Union (UIU). These took over from Odo-Okpoto in 1937, with Gabriel Ezekwo as the first chairman to serve as an administrative organ of the town. This structure grew to become the single most respected governmental authority in the community until recent times. The organisation instituted scholarship schemes for students, which led to the astronomical increase in the demography of educated indigenes within the first two decades of its existence.

The achievements of UIU cannot be conclusively enumerated without highlighting the infrastructural development and provision of public amenities undertaken by this organisation. They cleared bush paths; contributed to building churches; streamlined commercial activities at the Nkwo-Uchu market; stopped some unwholesome pagan practices; doused tension in times of rivalries between Christian denominations; helped attract the attention of the colonial government to the town for provision of amenities; and, most importantly, unanimously selected (from among them) the first traditional ruler for the community, in the person of HRH Igwe Ignatius Onyeneme Ofobuike MFR in 1966.

Gabriel founded and served the UIU as its first president-general for ten years, before becoming patron and life patron. He served the union with other illustrious sons of the town, like Sir William Ibeneme Ojiakor of Osete village who was the union's pioneer secretary and later served as its president-general. A trailblazer in his own right, Sir W.I. Ojiakor followed in the footsteps of Gabriel to provide leadership to the union and worked to sustain and stabilise it until the selection of a paramount ruler.

Through constant consultations with Gabriel Ezekwo, Chief Sir W.I. Ojiakor and Igwe I.O. Ofobuike led Umuchu as its first traditional prime minister and paramount ruler respectively.

Within the period of about four decades, the UIU blossomed into a formidable institution that bound together all sons and daughters of Umuchu both at home and abroad in a fraternal relationship that gave different segments and quarters of the confederating villages a sense of belonging.

The era could best be described as the glorious era of peace and development in Umuchu. The institution he founded and nurtured soon became a conglomerate of several unions comprising Umuchu citizens wherever they may be, with UIU branches established in almost all the major cities in Nigeria. Representatives were also drawn from various villages and clans in Umuchu. And all of them regularly contributed to the development of the town. Just to remember a few: Jeremiah Udechukwu Emenike, son of Emenike Orachusi of Ugwuakwu, was the chairman of UIU, Jos branch between 1944 and 1950; Chief Boniface Anusionwu Ezechukwu was at one time the chairman of Onitsha Branch; Lady Cecilia Udigwe Osuorah was the chairperson of UIU (women's wing) Lagos branch for many years; and Chief P.C. Ume-Akunne was also the first chairman UIU in the United Kingdom by 1955.

The UIU built and rehabilitated schools, renovated the stalls at Nkwo market, built town halls in places like Onitsha, and commenced a town hall project in Umuchu, etc. until the unfortunate leadership and political crises that engulfed the town between 1979 and 1983.

During this period there was also a rapid growth

of education and learning in the town, leading to the increase in the population of an elite class. Difference in political affiliation and leadership sentiments soon brought this large chunk of elite populace into a collision course with each other, leading to the balkanisation of the union during the second republic.

At this time of great upheaval, it was some of this second generation of the educated class who passed through Gabriel's mentorship that actually stepped in and resolved the impasse, not without the direction, guardianship and advice from their master: catechist Gabriel.

Notable among them were the Venerable C.A. Mbonu, Rev. Joshua Ezekwo, Rev. E. M. C. Egbunonu and other members of the famous Archdeacon Mbonu Peace Committee. The recommendations of the peace committee led to the establishment of a constitutional chieftaincy system in the town and the reformation of UIU, to become the fulcrum of political administration of the town.

Gabriel was always consulted in times of crises and the people trusted his right sense of judgment. His lucid advice in such times was like a soothing balm to troubled souls, which brought calm to the turbulent waters of life.

One such instance where he brought his wisdom to bear was during the selection process and consequent recognition of the first paramount ruler of Umuchu, Igwe Ignatius Onyeneme Ofobuike. Recall that Umuchu town consisted of semi-autonomous communities led by chiefs known as 'isiobis', united only by the mythical ancestral bond of 'Uchu', which existed in the subconscious mind of every citizen. To establish effective control of the fragmented Igbo societies, Umuchu included, the British colonial government sought to bring these clan heads into the colonial administration through issuance of recognitions to them by way of warrants. These warrant chiefs held sway in most villages despite their high handedness against their own people, sustained by the British overlords who ultimately benefited from their collation of taxes, levies and rates.

By the immediate post-colonial era, Umuchu still had seven functional warrant chiefs.

The post-civil war military administration had jettisoned the warrant chief system and any dealings with clan heads, through several local government reforms, which recognised town councils as against the dictates of chiefs. Yet the remnants of the vestiges of the warrant chief system continued to assert some level of authority in most communities and refused to accept the new realities.

By the 1976 local government reforms, each community was expected to elect a representative to the local government council. The UIU, under the leadership of Mr. B.A. Ezechukwu, selected Ide Gabriel Ezekwo as Umuchu's representative/counsellor to the old Aguata local government council. Gabriel humbly declined, giving the excuse of his age despite the fact that he was a member of the local government finance committee. Instead, he advised that younger persons be given the opportunity to test their mettle and garner experience in political leadership, as he was content with his advisory role in his position as life patron of UIU. Sir Basil Umuobieli Osuorah was subsequently elected as the counsellor for Umuchu town and representative at the local government council.

Meanwhile, following the local government reforms, the Anambra State government promulgated the chieftaincy edict of 1976. The military edict spelt out the processes for selection and recognition of paramount rulers for towns and communities, by dividing them into first-class, second-class, and third-class chiefs.[38]

The then chief information officer in Anambra State Ministry of Information, Mr. Godson Ezechukwu (now the traditional ruler of Umuchu), got hold of the new chieftaincy law, and quickly proposed to the UIU that Igwe Ignatius O. Ofobuike be recognised as the paramount traditional ruler of the town (first-class status), with the seven isiobis or their descendants as traditional rulers for other villages.

With this proposal, Godson O. Ezechukwu envisioned a big town with one paramount ruler and other chiefs to be recognised as traditional rulers, which can be equivalent to and can rub shoulders with the three ancient kingship institutions existing in Igbo land long before this time, namely the Obi of Onitsha, Eze-Aro and Obi of Oguta.[39] His suggestion no doubt was geared towards giving the town a new status, so it could attract other economic and infrastructural developments like Onitsha.

HRH Igwe Godson O. Ezechukwu wrote in his autobiography thus: "I made a suggestion to the Umuchu meetings that a new chieftaincy constitution be written to give some functions to descendants of the warrant Chiefs. My suggestion for a new constitution was interpreted as opposition to Chief Ignatius O. Ofobuike. To my surprise, both the Umuchu Improvement Union and town council chairman refused to sign the document."

No matter how plausible his intentions may have sounded, he was viewed with suspicious eyes. Antagonists to the proposition interpreted it as a covert move to elevate one of the strong contenders to the throne, the clan head of Ugwuakwu, Chief

Raphael Umezinwa, as a traditional ruler, and whittle down Igwe Ignatius O. Ofobuike's sphere of influence. Some interpreted it as an ambitious way of creating a constitutional role for descendants of the old warrant chiefs, considering that the genealogy of the proponent himself is traceable or linked to a former isiobi of Ozara-Akukwa, Chief Okparaogu Okparaeke.

His suggestion implied that being a descendant of a warrant chief, he could also be recognised as a traditional ruler. Well, being ambitious is still a virtue and not a vice. He was eventually crowned the traditional ruler of Umuchu, twenty-seven years later.

Meanwhile, his proposition brought much disagreement, "which nearly escalated into physical confrontation. Tempers were very high leading to exchange of harsh words, threats and the tearing of the union's minute book to pieces by [an] irate member."[40]

The rancorous situation that ensued threatened the unity of the once peaceful town. Citizens were divided between the supporters of Chief Ofobuike and Chief Umezinwa.

Chief Raphael Umezinwa instituted a legal action against Chief Ignatius Ofobuike asking the court to stop the state government from recognising the latter as the ruler of Umuchu.

The UIU became factionalised as well. Once again, the life patron of the town union, Ide Gabriel Ezekwo, became the rallying point of all peace moves as he intervened to find amicable resolution to the impasse.

The astute peacemaker engaged most of the dramatis personae and other relevant stakeholders to several parleys at his country home. Pa Gabriel maintained that Chief Ignatius Ofobuike was the best man for the throne at that period, having been selected earlier, in 1966, for the position. Ide Gabriel appealed to the disputants and their supporters to maintain the status quo. By his assessment, "Ofobuike is a clever man, handsome; stands tall with piercing bright eyes, radiating high intelligence. He will fight like [a] lion to get what belongs to Umuchu anywhere and anytime."[41]

This fair assessment was in tune with the general mood of the people, who wanted a paramount chief who was resourceful, enterprising, and capable of contending with other influential chiefs of neighbouring towns – like Chief Ugochukwu of Umunze, N.N. Anyika of Ezinifite, M.Z.C. Okpala of Achina, Duru Umuzinwa of Nkpologwu, Chief Ejidike of Agulu, and so on. "His personality, his outspokenness and wits were the qualities which endeared him to the majority of Umuchu people.

They found in him, the calibre of a man capable of projecting the image of the town to the outside world."[42]

During his lifetime, Igwe Ofobuike acknowledged more than once and publicly that the open endorsement of his candidature by the elder statesman, even in the face of stiff opposition, greatly encouraged and emboldened him to serve his people with every sense of purpose, commitment and diligence.[43]

As the leadership crises that rocked the UIU, indeed the entire town, continued up till 1983, men of goodwill like Ide Gabriel could no longer continue to remain silent or aloof, as the situation continued to degenerate.

Having retired from active public service and enjoying the status of a senior citizen, he became the rallying point for the second and third generation of educated elites in town. His modest stone house quickly became the meeting point of civil servants of Umuchu extraction, whenever they visited home.

The clergy among them would come to tap from the abundant experience of the pioneer church administrator while the teachers among them would converge at Ide's compound to inform him of the latest developments in the teaching profession. It was through this constant interface that Ide Gabriel succeeded in rallying together his disciples like Venerable C.A. Mbonu, Rev. J.C. Ezekwo and Rev. E. M. C. Egbunonu, who later invited other clerics and intelligentsias to form what was known as the Archdeacon Mbonu Peace Committee on which platform the hydra-headed crises were eventually resolved. After the amicable resolution of the thorny issues that plagued the town, Umuchu continued to enjoy real peace and brotherhood.

These worthy disciples that came together under the auspices of the Archdeacon Mbonu Peace Committee worked assiduously under the guardianship of their mentor and the pillar that held the town together. They practically brought to an end the period of mutual suspicion, rancour and acrimony.

For the benefit of the current generation, the issues that were at the core of the crises include the chieftaincy tussle between Chief Ofobuike and Chief Umezinwa, which started as far back as 1966, leading to the balkanisation of the UIU. The two factions of the union pitched tents on either side of chieftaincy tussle. Villages and age grades were not spared in this ugly trend, and villages were almost at war with each other. Soon the battleground shifted to the law court. The situation became worse during 1979 to 1982 and Nigeria's political dispensations when the town was literally torn to shreds by local political gladiators. All aspects of social interaction depended upon the political party one belonged to, either the Nigerian People's Party (NPP), which was in control of the government at the state level, or the National Party of Nigeria (NPN), which was in charge of government affairs at the federal level.

Meetings of the UIU degenerated to the level of acrimonious partisanship on issues of community development. The situation declined to the extent that there was a breakdown in the leadership of the union, leading to the resignation of Mr. Boniface Ezechukwu in 1983 as president general, and the unfortunate formation of parallel leadership. One was led by Raphael Orajiaka as president, while another group was led by Raphael Uzoigwe as president. While the former group declared tacit support for the candidacy of Chief Ofobuike in the chieftaincy tussle and the NPP-led state government, the latter aligned with Chief Umezinwa and NPN-led federal government. It was at the height of this squabble and schism that the elderly statesman and retired catechist called together his disciples who were in the clerical order that were known to be non-partisan and non-allied, to commence the process of unifying the people and restoring peace to the troubled town by finding an amicable solution to all the issues at stake. Gabriel, who was a nonagenarian by then, knew that he may not have the energy to personally intervene in the matter, but in his capacity as the pillar (ide) that supports the community, he could still act through other men of goodwill that he mentored. This was in line with the local Igbo adage that says that an elder cannot be at home and allow the goat to give birth while tied with a rope.

This challenging phase in the history of Umuchu from 1976 to 1986 no doubt brought some temporary setbacks to the once peaceful and progressive society. But the community quickly bounced back to the positive trajectory it was on before the impasse.

It is therefore pernicious and smacks of intellectual perfidy for anyone to hold that Umuchu was a broken society or ungovernable community before the inauguration of Umuchu Town Union Caretaker Committee in 1986 by the Ven. Mbonu-led group of peacemakers.

It is even more absurd when notable sons of the town peddle the vainglorious misinformation that the pre-1984 UIU was like a "market place for men" or that "the so-called constitution of UIU before the Archdeacon Mbonu Peace Committee Report was not much difference from a scrap."

This highly self-serving narrative, put forward by no less a person than Mr. T.O. Umeasiegbu, is to say the least a futile effort to thwart history and unduly massage the ego of the few surviving members of the Archdeacon Mbonu Peace Committee, while attempting to wipe out or belittle the immense contributions of other eminent sons and daughters of the town who had contributed towards the development of the town, from 1900 to 1983.

However, he could be forgiven, because Mr. T.O. Umeasiegbu has not featured in the activities or the process of social engineering of his hometown until 1984; therefore, he portrayed himself as being grossly ignorant of the facts of history. "He featured in the public affairs of Umuchu for the first time as a member of the Archdeacon Mbonu Peace Committee from January 1984 to January 1986".[44]

The true position of the history regarding the socio-political and administrative convolutions in Umuchu before the schism was that the UIU, which Gabriel Ezekwo founded in 1937, provided and strengthened the constitutional framework for the governance of the town as a traditional society. The cardinal objectives of the union were to promote love, unity and progress, as well as to pursue the socio-economic and cultural development of the community. Indigenes of the community who migrated to the big cities either for business, public service or education, also established branches of the union at their places of residence. Officers of the union were elected on fixed tenures through a well-spelled-out democratic process. Its meetings at all levels were conducted along modern procedures. Minutes of the meetings were carefully taken by the secretary, while the chairman presented the agenda for each meeting. Also, the financial officers kept all record of accounts and rendered the same whenever they were called upon to do so. The UIU meetings were very orderly. Only one person was mandated to speak at a time. The provost acting as the chief whip ensured that the meeting proceeded smoothly and in an orderly fashion.[45]

Another remarkable disagreement that affected this town during this period, in which Gabriel Ezekwo personally intervened, was the scramble for the establishment of a secondary school in Umuchu.

In the immediate post-civil war era, the government of east-central states had taken over the management of schools and asked communities that wanted to establish schools to donate land and build classroom blocks for the government to approve them as community secondary schools.

As a result of this policy, fifty-five new secondary schools built by communities were approved for public use on 4 November 1977 in the old Anambra State.

The people of Ozara-Akukwa village in Umuchu took advantage of this opportunity to rekindle their aspiration of having a post-primary school established in the area. This aspiration had been suspended in 1960, following the inability of the Catholic mission to conclude the building of the proposed Bishop Heerey's College project.

The chiefs, leaders and people of Ozara-Akukwa sought to convert the site to a secondary school. Structures were put up through levies and donations made by the villagers. Government approval was sought for the new school.

Unfortunately, this was the period of great division in Umuchu. The Catholic mission in Umuchu petitioned the government against the conversion of their property into a secondary school. In a letter dated 2 January 1978, leaders of the Roman Catholic Church warned against the takeover of the land "without authority and consultation."[46]

Gabriel rose to the occasion and engaged them on the need to allow the building of the secondary school, as it would benefit the entire people of Umuchu, rather than leaving the land to remain fallow with the uncompleted project of Bishop Heery's College.

In several of the meetings, Gabriel appealed to them to see the importance of the new project because the Catholic Church might never complete the old college project, as the new government policy on education no longer allowed churches to build, own and manage schools.

Gabriel and other well-meaning individuals were still battling to pacify the Catholic mission when HRH Igwe Ignatius Ofobuike wrote another petition to the government seeking to stop the approval of the proposed school being undertaken by Akukwa village.

In the letter dated 14 April 1978 and addressed to the honourable commissioner ministry of education and information, Enugu, HRH Igwe Ofobuike opposed the siting of a secondary school in the Ozara-Akukwa and asked education authorities not to approve the secondary school being proposed by the Akukwa people, and instead to approve the one being built jointly by the entire Umuchu people located at Okpu-na-Achalla village.

Indeed, the internecine strife and rivalry as a result of the Igweship tussle was again brought to the fore. HRH Igwe Godson Ezechukwu, who was then the coordinator of the school building project, described his predecessor's letter as a "highly damaging petition against his own community".[47]

When the information about the Igwe's petition was brought to the knowledge of Gabriel Ezekwo, probably by some Umuchu indigenes working in the ministry of education and information, he once again showed the courage and audacity to stand against what was wrong; speak the truth, not minding whose ox is gored.

In a swift reaction, Gabriel publicly lambasted Igwe Ofobuike in the presence of a Catholic congregation (which included HRH Ofobuike himself) on Sunday 25 June 1978. Gabriel Ezekwo informed the entire church that Igwe Ofobuike wrote a letter to the government of Anambra State against the siting of a secondary school at Akukwa stating that such move was a despicable act, which inhibited the progress of Umuchu as a whole.

In a letter by one Mr. Onwusiribe Chukwuka to his brother Christian Chukwuka and dated 4 July 1978, Mr. Chukwuka narrated how Gabriel orchestrated several meetings to harmonise and reconcile the conflicting issues hampering the smooth take-off of the new post-primary educational facility. It should be noted that Gabriel had summoned a think-tank meeting in his house that same Sunday at 3pm, where he impressed on Igwe Ofobuike to withdraw his petition against the school project, although the traditional ruler explained that he did what he did because the Akukwa people did not consult him before embarking on the project, which according to him was disdainful and a slight on his personality and office as the government-recognised paramount ruler of Umuchu. Others who were said to be present at the peace talk were: Chief Vitus Umetiti (chairman of the village building committee), Mr. Joel Ezeiheshie (Akukwa village treasurer), Mr. Ume Ezeanokwasa, Sir Simon Onunkwo etc.

Following this mediation and conciliation effort, as well as other interventions from several quarters, Igwe Ofobuike and the Catholic mission agreed to withdraw their opposition to the developmental strides of a people that were desirous of improving the dignity of man through education.

The school project was completed within six months and was immediately approved by the government as a technical school, while the one at Okpu-na-Achalla also gained approval as a secondary school, both on 18 September 1978, with a pioneer class intake of 160 students each. This huge number of students, mostly sons and daughters of Umuchu, as well as so many others that had or would still pass out from the schools, would have been denied the benefit of post-primary education because of a battle of egos by elders, most of whom have joined the ever-increasing league of ancestors.

What is instructive in this story is that Gabriel Ezekwo never failed to support any initiative that could bring development, unity, progress and peace for all humanity, which earned him the accolade 'a holy man of peace'.

He would say the blunt truth, even when it didn't go down well with some people, whether they were his relatives or friends. Gabriel exposed and chided Igwe Ofobuike when the latter erred, despite the fact that both were allies, considering that the latter became paramount ruler through the nomination and support of the former.

It was in appreciation of his pioneering effort as well as his undisputed position as a pathfinder in the development of his community that Igwe-in-council, Isiobi-in-council, the UIU (Home and Abroad), and the leadership of all existing age grades unanimously recognised him as the founder and father of modern Umuchu, and bestowed on him the title of 'Ide 1', which literally means 'the pillar or foundation of Umuchu'. This was a huge honour he would have humbly declined, save for the intervention of the archbishop on the Niger, Rt. Rev. Dr. Jonathan Onyemelukwe, who convinced him to accept the honour from his beloved town.

His initial refusal was born out of his nature of simplicity and humility, not being keen on things that showcased flamboyancy or exhibition of wealth in whatever form. It is based on this that the leadership of the community, led by the Igwe I. O. Ofobuike, agreed to foot the bills of all items and regalia needed for the chieftaincy ceremony. Indeed, it was a true recognition from the people and by the people, unlike many nowadays who it is believed spend a fortune to buy up titles from communities just for the sake of showmanship.

In his humble manner, Gabriel Ezekwo didn't use the titular prefix 'Chief' or refer to himself as such, but chose to be addressed as simply Ide Gabriel N. Ezekwo.

Speaking of the title bestowed on Gabriel, Igwe G. O. Ezechukwu maintained that Gabriel Nnolim Ezekwo would remain the only one in annals of the community to be honoured and referred to as Ide 1. This, he stressed, was because there can only be one foundation that carries the community, as multiplicity of Ides or foundations would result to the proverbial situation of "too many cooks spoil the broth". Meaning that if there were to be many foundations, the house (Umuchu) would have collapsed or would one day sink like rubble.

Hence, in Ide Gabriel Ezekwo, Umuchu people have broken the pattern that has prevailed in most Igbo communities of repetitive titular nomenclatures, because a particular title cannot be granted to another person due to its significance in the existence of the people, as well as the special position of relevance or contributions of the honoree to the development of his community.

Similar to this was the naming of 1.6 kilometre stretch of road between Achina-Umuchu boundary to Nkwo Umuchu junction as 'Ide Gabriel N. Ezekwo Road', following the approval granted by the Aguata Local Government Council in November 2018.

The local government authorities were quick to grant the request considering the level of patriotism exhibited by Ide Gabriel Ezekwo and the place of pride the name occupies in the memory of the people. The road was commissioned on 13 December 2018 by HRH Igwe G. O. Ezechukwu, supported by the chairman of Aguata Local Government Area, Hon. Eche Ezeibe. Also in attendance were the president general of UIU, Barr. Amos Ezejesi; Ven. David Obiagboso, the archdeacon of St. Thomas' Anglican Church Umuchu; Hon. Victor Umeh, the counsellor representing Umuchu ward two in Aguata Local Government Area; the head of works Aguata Local Government Area, Engr. Peter Ekwobi, and so many others.

The trustee of the foundation has since commenced routine maintenance and desilting of drainages along the road, to ensure its preservation for public good.

Similarly, Umuchu Improvement Union Representative Assembly (UIURA), and

Igwe-in-council approved erecting the statue of Ide Gabriel Ezekwo on the grounds of Umuchu town centre to honour him as the founder of UIU, the Umuchu government.

The difference between leadership and statesmanship is that leaders are known, while statesmen are remembered. Leaders are known by their achievements when alive or while occupying a leadership position. On the other hand, statesmen are remembered long after their demise, for touching people's lives during their lifetime. Leaders live by their glory while statesmen live eternally in people's memory. This synchronises with the thoughts of former president of United States Abraham Lincoln, when he posited that politicians think of the next election, while statesmen think of the next generation.

The current outpouring of honours and recognitions on Gabriel Ezekwo places him undisputedly among the league of statesmen.

In Amaraku, Isi Ala-Mbano Local Government Area of Imo State, the chiefs and people of the town still remember the invaluable contributions Gabriel Ezekwo made to the development of the area during his missionary evangelism as far back as 1943.

He is the missionary teacher who was reputed for building the 'road' that brought development to Amaraku and instrumental in the demolition of the existing St. Ebenezer CMS church earlier built with mud and raffia, and swiftly completed the first concrete church building that was dedicated by Rt. Rev. C. J. Patterson, the then bishop of diocese on the Niger on 31 August 1946. The new church was renamed St. Peter's Anglican Church and became a model structure that marked the beginning of a new era in construction of modern architecture in the area, with blocks, cement and zinc roofs.

He built new classroom blocks for the central school Amaraku and the then education secretary of Niger diocese, Mr. G.E.I. Cockin, came for inspection and approval for the school to commence standards one to four classes.[48] With this upgrade from elementary status to primary school status, there was great increase in education and enlightenment in the area. Gabriel literarily showed the light and the people embraced it to find their way into modernity.

In his memory, the chiefs and people of Amaraku, led by HRH Eze Joseph Chinyereze Mbamara, conferred on his first son, Chief (Engr.) Samuel Ezekwo, the honourary chieftaincy title of Ogbuhuru-Uzo on 26 December 2017. Ogbuhuru-Uzo translates to mean pathfinder/inventor, showing that the people of Amaraku were still savouring the great banquet of development and enlightenment prepared by God's servant.

HRH Eze Mbamara of Amaraku conferring High Chieftaincy
title to Chief Samuel Ezekwo on 26 December 2017

Friends of Gabriel Ezekwo pose with the family after
conferment of posthumous awards to late Ide Gabriel
and wife at Immanuel Anglican Church, Nawfija
on 31 December 2017

Similar to this was another posthumous award given to the late Ide Gabriel Ezekwo by the entire pastors and laity of the Anglican Communion in Nawfija mother parish on 31 December 2017, in recognition of his outstanding legacies to the growth of Immanuel Anglican churches, development of the community and education of its people.

Family and friends of the Ezekwos chatted at Immanuel Church Nawfija with nostalgia after the conferment of a posthumous award on the late Ide and Mrs. Gabriel Nnolim Ezekwo.

Expertise in conflict resolution is a necessary skill for a good community leader. Gabriel was richly endowed with this scarce expertise with the needed goodwill to push through, and he deployed it creditably for the benefit of the various communities he served.

Chief Fredrick Nnanna Nnorum told the investigator, "I remember an incident when my father's half-brother, Josiah Nwagwuisi, who was a serving member of the church committee, fell down and broke his arms during the renovation of the church leaking roof. The church members present brought him to our house. But my father in anger brought out his Dane gun to shoot them, lamenting that he willingly gave them land for their religion, but they turned around to take the life of his brother.

Gabriel Ezekwo was alerted and he intervened. It was through personal pleadings laced with jokes that Ezekwo was able to pacify my angry father. Ezekwo assured him that the church would take care of his injured brother. The catechist lived up to this promise through a local physiotherapist who was contracted to treat the fractured bone, until the wounded arm completely healed. That helped to build confidence among the rest of the family members leading to their total conversion and acceptance of the CMS church." Chief F.N. Nnorom claimed that, "Although my father remained a heathen (Ama-Ala) till death, Ezekwo converted all our family to Anglican. Today, my family is the largest single Anglican family in Amaraku."[49]

His insatiable thirst for community development through peaceful co-existence of all humans was again brought to bear when he served at St. John's Church located at Obodo village, Amaimo community of Ikeduru Local Government Area of Imo state.

Here, the famous catechist founded the 'Aladimma' Village Meeting. Both eighty-five-year-old Benniah Agwuka and eighty-six-year-old Sir Godwin Mmaduwuba confirmed knowledge of this legendary footprint at Amaimo. The Aladimma village meeting was a socio-political and economic association of mature adults, who help to settle interpersonal squabbles of all sorts and explore avenues of developing their community.

Aladimma, (meaning 'the land is good') was a clarion call to all male adult citizens to contribute their quota towards the collective good of all and by so doing make the land a better place for all her people. The town hall meeting was held on Nkwo-Ala market days. The group later metamorphosed into an economic pressure group that could mobilise funds from indigenes both at home and abroad in order to execute various development projects in the community.

The Aladimma meeting, which Gabriel instituted for the entire town, has since decentralised into smaller village groups, in line with current divisions of the larger community into small autonomous communities.

St. John's Church, where Gabriel served, is now located within Obodo community, and the community's version of the village meeting is called Onyemegbulaibeya (which translates as 'live and let live'). Through this platform, the community has attracted several development projects from government and donor agencies for the welfare of the people.

Pa Gabriel Ezekwo was often involved in settling land disputes in communities where he served, as such disputes would certainly hinder development. In Umuomaku, he helped to resolve the inter-village conflict that arose between Umuokpurukpu and Okpobe villages that would have caused a great disunity in the town on the issue of where to locate their central market, Eke. Three villages had their own markets: Umunambu, Nkwo; Okpobe, Afo; and Umukpurukpu, Eke. It was resolved that only one central market be approved. It was further agreed to site it at Okpobe and call it Eke Umuomaku.

Via the system of church and community collaboration, catechist Gabriel was able to bring about harmonious co-existence, good human interactions, and constant cross-fertilisation of ideas through grass-root dialogues, which engendered enduring peace, tranquillity and progress in any land in which he set his foot. By creating these human institutions, conflict resolution and crisis management in local communities became seamless to the extent that even the blind could bear witness that he built cities for God in conformity with the precepts of De Civitate Dei, as espoused by the fifth-century philosopher-cum-theologian St. Augustine of Hippo.

Human Capacity Development

Emerging in 1930 as the most educated person in Umuchu, the burden of mentorship was unequivocally to Gabriel. This position he assumed with great optimism. He set out to establish a platform that engendered the rise of a new generation of an educated class that could fit into the emerging colonial economy of the twentieth century and beyond.

An online weekly magazine recorded that the formation of Umuchu town union meeting was, in 1937, "when Chief Gabriel Ezekwo of Umuojogwo, Amanasaa-Umuchu blazed the trail by summoning a general meeting of all Umuchu male adults. A meeting of similar nature initiated earlier by the same man had rocked the boat. According to Chief Gabriel Ezekwo, hardly had he convened the meeting of the first failed attempt when some Ndi-ichie (High Chiefs) Ndi-Nze-na-Ozo (titled men) and other highly placed personalities turned it into a mini-customary court thereby negating the essence of its establishment. Worse still, more often than not, justice was perverted. As a result of this abnormality and deviation, he dissociated himself from this clique of profiteers called 'Odo-Okpoto' meeting and he summoned a new general meeting in December 1937. At the general meeting, Chief Gabriel Ezekwo was unanimously elected chairman. Chief Ezekwo made it abundantly clear that the aim of the meeting was not to perform any adjudicatory function but to coax Umuchu sons and daughters into going to school and acquire education as Gabriel learnt from people of other towns where he was then working as a school teacher."

Under the auspices of this group, Gabriel Ezekwo established an education scholarship scheme, through which the meeting mobilised resources to pay for indigent students of the town who were interested in furthering their studies at various high schools/colleges scattered all over the big cities of Onitsha, Umuahia, Enugu and Lagos. With this incentive, Ide Gabriel was able to raise a mass of high school and college students from the community. Their tuition fees were paid from the contributions he gathered from the meeting.

This scholarship scheme was so successful that by the 1950s and 60s, as the number of students under this scholarship scheme increased, the meeting shifted emphasis to university education and started sponsoring university undergraduates to premier institutions like the University of Ibadan and University of Nigeria. By this period, Umuchu town, through this scholarship, had sponsored several intelligent boys to acquire higher education abroad and in Nigeria's institutions of higher learning. The first beneficiary of the undergraduate scholarship scheme was Mr. Clement C. Nnolim. He was the first university graduate from Umuchu.

In his lifetime, Gabriel could count off the top

of his head tens of people that had benefited from the education incentive, who later grew to become highly influential members of society. Such people need not be mentioned here, as some may not like their poor background, or that their rise to affluence was sequel to community efforts as their indigent parents couldn't solely finance their secondary and higher education, to be made public.

Yet it must be made abundantly clear that virtually all the first crop of high school/college or university graduates from Umuchu were products of this scholarship programme, which was developed and administered by Ide Gabriel Ezekwo as part of his human capital development initiative. Most of the town's young people in various educational institution in the 1940s, 50s and 60s were supported by this education scholarship scheme.

However, tribute must be paid to all the adult male citizens of Umuchu, who contributed their scarce resources into the pool of funds that changed the lives of many people and turned around the fortunes of many families in the town. The people must be appreciated for having confidence in the pioneer leader of UIU, Ide Gabriel, and entrusting their meagre resources to his care. He (Gabriel) did not disappoint them, as he administered the union's funds for ten years, unblemished.

As part of his mentorship drive, Gabriel founded also the Anglican Teachers' Union in 1960, aimed at supporting and mentoring younger teachers, who were just coming out or still studying at various teacher training colleges.

As he was building a generation of educated elite in Umuchu, he was replicating the same feat simultaneously in his in-laws' town, Umuomaku, as well as various other towns where he had the opportunity of serving either as catechist or teacher.

From the religious standpoint, the church has a divine mandate to give true religious education to her converts. "Education is meant to prepare man for life. Our life begins in the world where [sic] generally last less than one hundred years. It continues in the next world where it lasts forever. Education must prepare man for a successful life in both."

Since religion without education tends to degenerate to superstition, Gabriel strove to spread Christianity and education in every town or village within his sphere of influence. He spared no labours in attracting and teaching young people in schools, as a kind of solid foundation for the Christian faith that he came to propagate. Even in the immediate post-civil war era, when government had taken over the management and control of schools, Gabriel continued to monitor the activities of teachers in the

Anglican schools to ensure that they were impacting sound Christian religious knowledge to their pupils. To achieve this, he undertook periodic oversight visits to schools within his district, as was discovered in his diary writings.

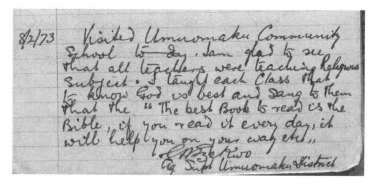

Pa Gabriel Ezekwo's logbook note

8/2/73

Visited Umuomaku Community School today. I am glad to see that all the teachers were teaching Religious subjects. I taught each class that to know God is best and sang to them that the "best Book to read is the Bible, if you read it every day, it will help you on your way, etc.

GN Ezekwo

Ag. Supt. Umuomaku District

With his amazing intuitive assessment of the peculiar situation of every community, Gabriel adopted a strategy that effectively brought more people to the church using the alluring merits of education as bait.

His house was a nest for young people who were desirous of getting formal education. At a time and age when most parents did not see the value of sending their children to school, or were too poor to afford the tuition, Gabriel personally facilitated and in some cases financed the education of many people. It could be said that providence placed him in the position of acting in loco parentis to many young people. He shouldered this responsibility with great enthusiasm.

Mention must be made of Archdeacon Christopher Mbonu, who Gabriel converted to Christianity, encouraged to go to school and mentored in Christian evangelism, until he (Mbonu) grew to become a church teacher and was later ordained a priest in 1955. At one point, he was the Archdeacon of Nnewi. Venerable Mbonu's parents remained heathens and did not see the need for Western education. They converted to Christianity after their son had become the first indigenous priest of the Anglican Church from Umuchu.

The second Anglican priest of Umuchu origin, Rev. Joshua Chukwunenye Ezekwo, also passed through Gabriel's tutelage. Both were cousins of Gabriel.

In 1931, when Gabriel started work as a church teacher in Umuduru district, he took young Joshua along with him. Joshua followed the footsteps of his mentor by becoming a church teacher, a catechist and later a priest. It is remarkable that Rev. Joshua not only took after Gabriel as a church teacher-cum-catechist, but also worked in some of the churches where Gabriel had served many years earlier. Rev. Joshua served as a catechist at St. John's church Osina from 1964 to 1966 where Gabriel also served in the 1930s. Similarly, Rev. Joshua served at Immanuel Anglican Church Nawfija for five years, many years after Gabriel had left the town.

When the young Joshua left Gabriel's household in 1935 for further studies Christian Nwokedike Ezekwo replaced him in 1938 as Gabriel's house-help following the birth of Gabriel's first daughter, Comfort (now Mrs. Comfort Anyikwa). Christian Ezekwo also followed the footsteps of the master and grew to become a church teacher. He lived and schooled under Gabriel from 1939 to 1952.

Another person that is worthy of mention is Mr. Simon Mmadunwuba Ezeani, who Gabriel took under his fatherly custody from 1959 to 1963 and ensured that he completed his standard six education before he trained as a technician, specialising in electrical and electronic works. He remained grateful to his mentor for providing him with the initial tools of trade after his training.

Gabriel also took custody of some of his brothers-in-law, such as Nathan Iloka. Gabriel facilitated his education up to Bishop Lasbury Teachers' Training College at Owerri. Upon completing his teacher training, Nathan returned to Gabriel's household at Nawfija, where Gabriel helped to secure a teaching appointment for him at Immanuel Anglican Primary School where Gabriel was both headmaster and church catechist.

Other in-laws who drank from Gabriel's milk of human kindness included Moses Iloka, Ifeoma Akanegbu and a host of many others. These were just a handful of the numerous people who are still living that saw the light of God and became liberated through the goodwill of Ide Gabriel in his lifetime. The consequential effect was improved living conditions for these individuals, as well as their various families, which were lifted out of poverty and ignorance.

Samuel Ezekwo recalled how he benefited from the advice his father was giving out to numerous young people that usually converged in their living room to drink from Gabriel's overflowing fountain of knowledge during his mentoring sessions. He stated that he became fascinated with studying engineering following the discussion between his father and an engineering student, Japhet Ezenwanne from Ezinifite, Aguata Local Government Area. Mr. Ezenwanne later became an engineer working for National Electric Power Authority (NEPA).

Family Values

Family values involve all the ideas of how one wants to live a good family life and they are often passed down from generation to generation. They help to define behavioural patterns in every situation as well as help youths make good choices and solidify the bond of family.

Gabriel promoted good Christian family values in all the places he worked and lived in his lifetime.

In Nawfija, for instance, Chief Eric Onyeagba paid glowing tribute to Ide Gabriel Ezekwo for introducing marriage-counselling sessions for wedded couples in the area. The octogenarian told the investigator that because of his good rapport with the people, most parents wanted him to be godfather to their children during baptism. As such he was the godfather and spiritual director to many young people in Nawfija, including his own son, Joel Onyeagba.

This marriage counselling helped to improve the moral life of Christian couples and increase family bonding among the faithful. According to Chief Eric Onyeagba, "The counselling sessions impacted positively on family values so much so that neighbouring communities like Ufuma adopted it. It is regrettable that such system of value re-orientation is no longer in practice in the church today, which has led to increase in marital crises and related vices among couples, leading to adultery, divorces and broken homes, that is currently pervading our society."

Together with his wife, Mercy, (who was a 1935 graduate of the famed St. Monica's women's college, Ugwuoba) they engaged couples in heart-to-heart discussions aimed at impacting good family values, for the betterment of the family unit and society at large. While Gabriel conducted this moral instruction through the fathers' union and the town unions that he founded, his wife, Madam Mercy, gathered women through the mothers' union for similar counselling sessions.

A retired headmaster, Pa Alford Chukwujioke Ukaigwe, recounted how catechist Ezekwo and his wife made the title "Mrs." become the exclusive preserve of wedded women in Nawfija and its environs. This beautiful and prestigious title made most women compel their husband to wed them in the church, so as to be addressed as Mrs.

To encourage Christian marriages, betrothed young women underwent training sessions on how to be a good homemaker and housewife and perform other roles expected of women in Christian marriage.

The home of the catechist was the training ground for young couples and an arbitration house for the settlement of marital problems. It was in this area that Mrs. Mercy Ezekwo actually deployed her skills and learning from the women's college where she schooled. This phenomenal catechist did not just 'talk the talk', but also 'walked the talk'. He did not just preach these moral precepts but he lived by them.

According to Pa Stephen Nwagalaku, by living out what they preached, Gabriel and his wife became a shining example to many families in Nawfija.

During his long stay in the community, Gabriel reduced drastically acts of treachery, back-biting and gossips both in the families and in the church groups.

Anytime someone came to lay a complaint against another person, the catechist would immediately send for the accused to come and hear the complaint brought against him/her, personally. In this way both the accuser and the accused would talk over the matter eyeball to eyeball.

Gabriel tried not to leave any communication gap for rumours or gossips to fill. Thus, interpersonal conflicts based on gossips and falsehood were curtailed to their barest minimum, as any accuser must be ready to confront the accused with facts and figures not rumours or falsehood.

Church Administration

Church administration is part of the service rendered to the body of Christ, which entails the wise stewardship of God's resources for the accomplishment of the work of Christian ministry. Administration is not an end in itself, but rather it is a means for serving people effectively while making efficient use of available resources in a manner that uplifts the body of Christ on Earth in a manner that glorifies God, in heaven above. Therefore, God is honoured and believers are encouraged when church affairs are administered well. Hence, church administrators should be spiritually mature and able to work well with other church leaders as a group, as well as with the entire congregation, as one body of Christ.

In his days, Ide Gabriel Ezekwo exhibited exceptional skills in church administration. He deployed his energy and time in various spheres of discipleship like prayers, preaching and teaching. This colossus did not only excel in these core areas of his Christian vocation but he was, indeed, prudence and accountability personified.

Few persons who still have memories of him have maintained that Gabriel was a genius in the frugal and judicious application of lean resources to church programmes and projects, for maximum utility.

He was sagacious in adapting available means to achieve desired ends, which explained why people didn't hesitate to give out their widow's mite in support of any cause or project Gabriel wished to embark on. Wherever he went, people, both Christians and non-Christians alike, reposed so much confidence in him. And he didn't betray this enormous trust once.

Even the heathens in Umuchu had to abandon the Odo-Okpoto meeting as soon as Gabriel founded the UIU and a cross-section of the community contributed resources, time and physical strength in building the St. Thomas stone church, additional classroom blocks and other developmental projects in the area. This typified the level of trust he elicited from the people.

To date, the Anglican community in Nawfija is still surprised about how the catechist managed to pay off the accumulated church dues standing against Immanuel Church as a result of the financial imprudence of his predecessors in office.[50]

In Immanuel Church Ezinifite, Gabriel instituted the culture of savings and accountability. He constructed a heavy metal safe box, affixed permanently to the wall of the parsonage, where catechists lived. The catechist and the church treasurer handled the keys to the safe box and rendered accounts of the finances when needed.[51]

On account of frequent transfer of the keys from one catechist to another and from one treasurer to another, the keys to the safe box were lost. But the safe box exists to this day at the old parsonage of Immanuel Church Ezinifite, Aguata Local Government Area of Anambra State. This is one of the tangible legacies that is still standing to the memory of Ide Gabriel Ezekwo.

It is hereby suggested that the leadership of Aguata Anglican diocese should ensure that the box is unlocked and the contents kept in an archive or museum for the sake of posterity.

Ide Gabriel Ezekwo had a very good grasp of the basic tenets of Anglicanism. He had cause to display his mastery of the rules, while shepherding God's flock at St. Mary's Umuomaku, as recounted by Pa Augustus Onyenwa Nwakaife. He exhibited an uncommon ingenuity in the management of church funds after a communion service, on a certain Sunday. Usually after such services the presiding vicar takes home the offertory. But on that particular Sunday Gabriel used the church funds to buy the bread and wine used for the Holy Communion. After the service, the visiting pastor, Rev. C.C. Odilorah, asked for the offertory. The catechist politely educated him that he (the visiting pastor) could only take the offertory if he provided the items for communion, but as it was the church that provided those items, the proceeds of the offertory would go back to the church purse. "All of us in the church committee as at then, were stunned at his level of knowledge of church rules, courage and fearlessness and we learnt a big lesson from him on that day."[52]

His dexterity and precision in accurate record keeping and fiscal responsibility was simply exceptional, if not legendary, considering he had little or no knowledge of accounting or financial analysis. His arithmetical accuracy in financial calculations as contained in his file discovered in the archives of St. Mary's Church Umuomaku, showed that he was indeed a very meticulous church administrator.

His enigmatic capacity to evangelise, mobilise, organise, administer and nurture small CMS groups into big Anglican congregations was acknowledged by several church leaders through their various recorded testimonies.

Also, his indelible footprints in the sands of time, which are conspicuous in his many signature projects scattered all over the communities and churches that he worked, bear eloquent testimonies that a man of great vision and mission once upon a time passed through this world stage.

Even when it seemed as if there was, and there is still, a prevailing institutional conspiracy not to ascribe honours and achievements to lay evangelists, and rather all missionary breakthroughs be credited to the glory of men in the ecclesiastical order, yet the diocese on the Niger could not close its eyes to the unbeatable record of service this great soldier of Christ staring them on the face. His monumental achievements compelled the diocesan curia to elevate him to the status of district superintendent in 1972, a position that was hitherto the exclusive preserve of senior pastors who presided over a parish with other churches attached to it.

Gabriel presided over the affairs of St. Mary's Parish Umuomaku as district superintendent until his eventual retirement. He took over the management of the district from no less a person than the then archdeacon of Enugu, Venerable H.I. Okechukwu. The district had three other churches in neighbouring communities affiliated to it, namely St. James' Agbudu, St. Andrew's Enugu-Umuonyia and St. John's Anglican Church in Oneh. The aged Gabriel was saddled with the task of administering these four churches in the immediate post-civil war era.

What else would have informed the choice of Mr. Gabriel Ezekwo as a district superintendent other than his record of achievements and in-depth experience in Christian evangelism, church administration, and financial management as well as community mobilisation?

He represented the district in all the diocesan synods during his period of stewardship.

Mr. Gabriel Nnolim Ezekwo alongside other laymen of God took over and sustained the CMS mission in Igbo land after expatriate missionaries were forced to leave the southeast region based on the circumstances of the Nigeria-Biafra civil war. They not only sustained the missionary legacies like churches, schools and hospitals, but they also worked hard to entrench the Anglican Communion in the southern part of Nigeria, despite all the odds. Yet they have all been forgotten, as their legacies have almost been wiped out from living memory.

The least the church could do for those of the calibre of Gabriel who acquiesced to be subjected to a life of poverty and deprivation just to advance Anglicanism is to remember and immortalise them with memorials, plaques or structures in their names, in those areas they worked. It is utterly lamentable and totally regrettable, that these great soldiers of Christ are not even allowed to have a place in our dustbin of history. Nowadays, no one mentions them or makes any reference to their efforts whatsoever, just because we disdainfully look down on them for not passing through the formalities of ordination.

One of the greatest tributes that present church leaders could pay to these pioneers is to live out the true meaning or essence of their pastoral calling as a loud testimony to the current generation of faithful that the labours of our heroes past were not in vain.

Back home, in recognition of his outstanding contributions to the development of Umuchu, the leaders and people of the town unanimously bestowed on him the title of 'Ide' (meaning pillar/foundation) Umuchu, on 30 December 1982, an honour he had previously declined because of his Christian beliefs, which stemmed from his piety and humble background. It took quite some time and high moral persuasion from then bishop on the Niger, Rt. Rev. Dr. Jonathan Onyemelukwe, to convince Gabriel to accept the traditional honour from his own people.

Not until recently did the Anglican community in Nawfija honour Ide Gabriel Ezekwo and his wife, Lolo Mercy Ezekwo, with posthumous awards for their immense contribution to the growth of Christianity in the area and development of the town. The children of Ide Gabriel Ezekwo have relentlessly continued in the trajectory of sustaining the legacies of their father by immortalising the late sage.

The first son of the Ide Gabriel, Chief Samuel Ifeanyichukwu Ezekwo, has established a foundation in memory of their late patriarch.

Through the Ide Gabriel Nnolim Ezekwo Memorial Foundation, High Chief (Engr.) Samuel Ezekwo has undertaken the renovation of the St. Thomas stone church, Umuchu. The reconstruction was successfully carried out in 2019 and gave the old stone church a new look without distorting the original medieval-like architecture.

It is worthy of note that before the renovation effort, the stone church was already a shadow of itself. The building was used as a kindergarten school, later abandoned and no longer a place of worship as intended by the builders. The structure itself had dilapidated as the roof, foundation and stones were left to fall apart. In fact, it was nothing more than a playground for children, and a clear example of the poor maintenance culture pervading the Third World countries.

With the intervention of Chief Samuel Ezekwo, the church was completely gutted; the foundation/structures fortified; the building's roof and ceiling replaced; the floors tiled; the walls plastered and painted; and the old electrical system completely rewired and replaced with completely new fittings and fixtures. Thus the historic stone church was restored to its former glory.

The restoration effort was commissioned on 25 November 2018, by His Lordship Rt. Rev. Dr. Samuel Chukwudi Ezeofor JP, AMB. P. Bishop of Aguata

Diocese. Reading copiously from the Book of Haggai, Bishop Ezeofor prayed for God's greater glory to be restored upon the monument being rebuilt by Chief Samuel Ezekwo. Hence, Chief Samuel Ezekwo has obeyed the call to rebuild God's temple in Haggai 1:4 thus, "is it a time for you yourselves to dwell in your panelled house, while this house (temple) lies in ruins?"

The renovated stone church will henceforth be used as a memorial chapel and Umuchu Unity Centre for the benefit of all sons and daughters of the town. On the occasion, Bishop Ezeofor renamed the monument as 'Catechist Gabriel N. Ezekwo Memorial Chapel and Umuchu Unity Center'. It is symbolic of Umuchu unity and how the church and the community worked together for the development and welfare of the citizens in his days.

L-R: The rebuilt Catechist (Ide) Gabriel N. Ezekwo Memorial Chapel and Umuchu Unity Center and the new St. Thomas Anglican Church building

Ide Gabriel N. Ezekwo posing with his grandsons,
Obiajulu and Chukwuemeka in 1990

Ide Gabriel Nnolim Ezekwo in full chieftaincy regalia

Ide Gabriel N. Ezekwo

Ide Gabriel Ezekwo with his wife, Lolo Mercy Ezekwo in 1974. Retirement picture at Umuomaku

Ide Gabriel N. Ezekwo's wife, Lolo Mercy Ezekwo

Engr. Godson Ezekwo,
one of the three sons of
Ide Gabriel Ezekwo

Hon. Victor Ezekwo,
one of the three sons of
Ide Gabriel Ezekwo

Obiajulu and Becky

Becky poses with Gabriel and six-month-old Gabriella

Chief Samuel Ezekwo and wife; with two sons,
Obiajulu and Chukwuemeka

High Chief (Engr.) Samuel Ezekwo poses with family after
attending a Broadway show in New York City.
L-R: Emeka, Ifeoma, Obiajulu, Samuel

Mrs. Ozioma Ezeakunne (née Ezekwo) and family

Four of the five daughters of Ide Gabriel Ezekwo
L-R: Chinwe, Comfort, Ozioma, Chijioke

HRH G. O. Ezechukwu OON, (Igwe Umuchu) conferring chieftaincy title to High Chief (Engr.) Samuel I. Ezekwo on 30 December 2015

Cenotaph for 161 Umuchu soldiers who served during the Nigerian Civil War under construction by High Chief (Engr.) Samuel Ezekwo

HRH Eze Joseph Mbamara (Igwe Amaraku) presents High Chief Samuel Ezekwo his chieftaincy certificate on 26 December 2017

All the recipients of the cash award from Ide Gabriel Nnolim Ezekwo Memorial Foundation pose with High Chief (Engr.) Samuel Ezekwo, HRH G. O. Ezechukwu OON, Hon. Victor Ezekwo, Mrs. Ozioma Ezeakunne, etc., December 2016

HRH Godson O. Ezechukwu unveiling Ide Gabriel N. Ezekwo Road, Umuchu on 13 December 2018

Rt. Rev. Dr. Samuel C. Ezeofor (Bishop Diocese of Aguata) and High Chief (Engr.) Samuel I. Ezekwo pose with some of the attendees of the Catechist (Ide) Gabriel N. Ezekwo Memorial Chapel and Umuchu Unity Center, 25 November 2018

Mrs. Edith Odimegwu (née Ezekwo); the fifth daughter of
Ide Gabriel Ezekwo and family

Commissioning of Catechist (Ide) Gabriel N. Ezekwo
Memorial Chapel and Umuchu Unity Center by
Rt. Rev. Dr. Samuel Chukwudi Ezeofor, Bishop Diocese
of Aguata on 25 November 2018

Rt. Rev. Dr. Samuel C. Ezeofor, Bishop Diocese of Aguata
and High Chief (Engr.) Samuel I. Ezekwo pose together
after the commissioning ceremony on 25 November 2018

Unveiling of Ide Gabriel N. Ezekwo Road. L-R: Barr. Amos
Ezejesi, Ichie Chinedu Ezeuka, Chief Martin Okpala, High
Chief (Engr.) Samuel Ezekwo, HRH G. O. Ezechukwu
OON, Hon. Eche Ezeibe, Chief (Prof) Ifejirika, Hon. Victor
Umeh, Engr. Peter Ekwobi

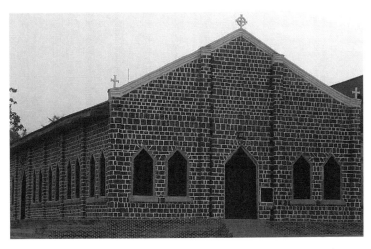

The rebuilt dilapidated Catechist (Ide) Gabriel N. Ezekwo Memorial Chapel and Umuchu Unity Center funded by High Chief (Engr.) Samuel Ezekwo

Dedication of public borehole water supply funded by High Chief (Engr.) Samuel Ezekwo on 13 April 2017 by the Most Rev. Dr. Christian O. Efobi, the Archbishop of Province of the Niger

Chapter Six

Anglican Evangelism in the Twenty-First Century

Ide Gabriel Nnolim Ezekwo was born in the late nineteenth century, spent his eventful life in the twentieth century, and transited in 1991, just at the dawn of the new age of globalisation.

Although he couldn't see the twenty-first century, missionaries in the ilk of Gabriel foresaw a future when the Anglican Communion would be well entrenched in all the villages and hamlets of the country, a golden era where there would be a church within a reasonable distance of all faithful.

While this has been achieved by the physical church structures that dot the entire landscape of Igbo land, there are some negative trends that are currently plaguing the Anglican Church in Nigeria, which Pa Gabriel and his contemporaries could not have anticipated.

According to Proverbs 14:28 and Acts 4:13, God is interested not just in the growth of the church, but also in the piety of every member of the church. Thus, Christians are expected to live out the true meaning of their creed. The increase in the expansion of Anglican churches in the southeast of Nigeria ought to correspond with increased interest in godliness and selfless services to humanity in order to ensure a peaceful and progressive society.

In both Matthew 5:13 and John 1:15, Christians are enjoined to live exemplary lives that can bring about a just society, which is why the scriptures described them as the light and salt of the earth. But from all indications, the reverse seems to be the case in Nigeria, when one considers the disturbing trend that the increase in churches has given rise to increased moral decadence in society and among the ecclesiastical order.

This ugly trend certainly negates the wishes and aspirations of past heroes of the church and soldiers of Christ who fought hard, even at the risk of their lives, to spread Christianity in the southeast and beyond.

The alarming rate of moral decadence in Nigerian Christianity could be regarded as the cumulative effects of the failure of many social institutions in Nigeria. These institutions include the family, school, churches etc. in contemporary Nigeria.

In the family, parents with sound moral and ethical sanctity are scarcely available as they were in traditional society. Hence, morally-decadent children are increasing by the day. When these children move from homes to educational institutions, they become worse due to the sorry state of the education in the country. Some of these young people later find themselves in our various seminaries, en route to becoming priests and pastors. If the formators and tutors at this level fail to carry out proper examination of the characters of the young aspirants, then they end up in the pulpits half baked.

In the churches, where moral values are expected to be inculcated, many strange practices and teachings have found their way into our religious doctrines. Many churches have come out strongly to condemn the immorality.

To combat the moral decadence, Churches have embarked on many commendable programs, including taking back many of their schools that were seized by the Government after the civil war and building new mission schools where students' code of conduct and morality are given highest priority. The churches also fund robust youth programs where they mentor and nurture the young people who will one day find their way to the church pulpits.

Despite the negative observations mentioned

above, and more, the solid foundation laid by the early evangelists like catechist Gabriel Ezekwo cannot be said to have been destroyed in the Anglican Communion. This is so because there is no other foundation that can be laid concerning the Church of Christ except on Jesus Christ. The Anglican Communion in Nigeria has maintained a steady growth, both spiritually and physically. Having resisted the introduction of strange doctrines into the Gospel of our Lord Jesus Christ by the Church of England, Anglican Communion, to a logical conclusion, bears an eloquent testimony to the fact that the Christian foundation is still intact.

The seeming increased rate of moral decadence in Nigerian Christianity stems from the fact that the Gospel of Christ is neither forceful nor coercive. Our Lord Jesus Christ, after teaching, will always say, "He who has ears to hear, let him hear". Acceptance and compliance is a question of choice. However, for the clergy, it is compulsory that they continue the line of the early evangelists who laboured for the Church's growth; and for the Church as a whole, the words of St Paul in his letter to Timothy in the second epistle, 2:19, is food for thought. Quote, "Nevertheless, the foundation of God stands sure, having this seal, the Lord knoweth them that are His, And let everyone that nameth the name of Christ depart from iniquity".

Appendix A
Memoir by Mrs. Ozioma Ezeakunne (née Ezekwo)

Our parents were good Christians who practised what they preached. My father used to call my mother 'sister' and my mother called him 'Nnanyi', which in English stands for 'our father'. They lived peacefully.

At the age of five years, my siblings and I had learned how to read the Bible. My mother used to train girls ready for marriage. These trainings consisted of Christian marriage, mannerisms, cooking, domestic house duties, reading and so on. In addition, I used to teach the other girls how to read the Bible.

My father had a bell to inform him about his food and once the bell was rung he would be aware that his food was served and ready. My father also used the same bell in the morning at 5am and evening at 8pm to make sure that everyone was aware of the time for morning and evening prayers. My parents allowed each of us to have turns leading and conducting prayers, by singing, reading passages from the Bible and prayers. We also attended morning and evening church services.

My parents bore four girls before the three boys, and my baby sister was the last of us, which made us now five girls. My father treated us all equally.

In those days, girls were not sent to school. People advised our father not to send the girls to school and to save money for the boys. Our father did not listen to the advice. Instead, he left it for us to decide what we wanted to do. One day, my father approached me and asked me if I wanted to go to school and I responded to him, saying, "Yes, I would love to continue my education."

He was ready to pay for my school tuition. He always had faith that God will provide. I studied hard and got into Ogidi Girls' boarding secondary school. To repay the opportunity I had been given by my father, I tried to economise at Ogidi Girls. My parents did not have money, but they sacrificed everything to make sure we got a good education. So I decided that I would help with my siblings' education.

After I graduated from Ogidi Girls, I was accepted at the University College Hospital, Ibadan as a nursing student. As a student, we were paid and given free board. I used the money I earned as a student to help my father pay for my siblings' tuition. My father was very grateful for the help and he used to call me 'Ozinwam' (Ozioma my child).

After the Biafra Nigerian war ceased, my father quickly came home from Uga, where he was teaching, to Umuchu and called me aside to tell me how my brother Samuel had taken his younger brother Godson with him and fled the country by plane to Gabon. My father said that Samuel had told him and my mother that he would leave Nigeria by any means, even by hanging on the tyres of a plane, if we lost the war, but they never believed him.

Before the war ended, Godson was staying with me at Awomama and was working with the Red Cross. Two weeks before the war had ended, Godson and the rest of his colleagues were let go. Godson went to Uga and that was how he was able to leave the country with Samuel. I told my father not to worry because those countries recognised Biafra and that they would take care of them, and moreover we didn't know what General Gowon would do with the Igbos. Some speculated that he would massacre the surviving Igbos.

My father believed in Christian marriage. When any of us were getting married, our father gave us the list of things that will help us in a happy Christian marriage.

Papa was ahead of his time in healthy living and he practised it. He never drank alcoholic drinks or smoked/sniffed/chewed tobacco. He worked out in the gym regularly with his students; he ate good food and insisted on having his dinner before 6pm. He loved bread fruit (ukwa), pounded yam, and other vegetables and vegetable-based food. He would not mind having ukwa every day. I remember when our mum was at Amaimo hospital to have a baby. Papa was alone without her cooking ukwa for him. One day when I came back from school, I saw Papa on his knees getting fresh ukwa seeds ready for cooking. I was shocked that he would do that. But he missed not having ukwa for a couple of days so he decided to help himself.

Appendix B
About the Author

Samuel Ifeanyichukwu Ezekwo is the first son of Ide Gabriel Nnolim Ezekwo.

During the Nigeria civil war, he served as a Military Intelligence Officer in the Biafran Army.

In 1970, at the end of Nigeria civil war, Samuel Ezekwo escaped from Nigeria to Gabon after the surrender of Biafran Army.

In 1971 he migrated from Ivory Coast to the United States of America where he earned Masters degree in Chemical Engineering from Columbia University, in the City of New York.

In 1976, he joined the British Petroleum in United States and worked as a Chemical Engineer at the Corporate Headquarters. While working for British Petroleum, he went to pilot school and took up flying single-engine aircrafts as a hobby.

Later, Samuel Ezekwo joined the United States Federal Government as a manager of remedial projects.

He is a contributor to a 2016 book titled *The Advent Of Christianity In Umuchu: (Achievements and Challenges) 1916 – 2016.*

He retired from United States Federal Government in 2016 and founded Ide Gabriel

Nnolim Ezekwo Memorial Foundation. As the Chairman, he positioned the charity organization to continue his late father's work in southeast Nigeria communities where his father served as a missionary.

Appendix C
About the Co-Author

Ejiofo Umegbogu is a justice of the peace, diplomatic historian, multi-disciplinary researcher, investigative journalist and civil society activist.

Mr. Umegbogu holds a B.A. (Hons) in history and international studies from Nnamdi Azikiwe University, Awka. He is a senior news reporter/editor at Federal Radio Corporation of Nigeria (Radio Nigeria) with special training from the Premium Times Centre for investigative journalism.

Appendix D
Request for Memoirs and Pictures

Biography of Ide Gabriel Nnolim Ezekwo
Sunday, May 21 2017, 6:07pm, Samuel Ezekwo

Happy Sunday Everybody;

Early this year I called for and received proposals from three teams of Investigative Journalists/Historians to conduct research and gather information on our late father's life and work in Imo and Anambra States.

During my one month visit to London to spend time with my grandson, I used the opportunity to deliberate and evaluate the proposals. I am happy to inform you that I have selected a team of investigative journalists/historians whom I believe will produce all necessary information that will be needed to write a biography of Ide Gabriel Nnolim Ezekwo.

As part of this project, they will contact you in due time and ask you to submit your memoirs on your personal relationship and knowledge of this icon, Pa Gabriel Ezekwo.

With all good wishes.
God is faithful.
Ide

Biography of Ide Gabriel Nnolim Ezekwo
Sunday, June 11 2017, 11:57am, Samuel Ezekwo

Happy Sunday Everybody.

Further to my email to you on 21st May 2017 regarding the subject matter, please submit your memoirs on your personal relationship and knowledge of our late father to me by 15th September 2017.

The present schedule for completion of the research into our late father's life calls for your memoirs to be received by me on the above date. DO NOT MISS OUT!!!!

Cheers.
God is faithful.
Ide

Ide Gabriel Ezekwo Biography: Request for pictures.
Friday, March 30 2018, 2:21pm, Samuel Ezekwo

Hi Everyone,

Write up of Ide Gabriel Ezekwo biography is progressing timely.

By this email, I invite each of you to send me an electronic copy of your family picture which will be part of the chapter on "Ide Gabriel Ezekwo DYNASTY".

I need to have the pictures on or before 15th May 2018.

Happy Easter,
Chief (Engr.) Samuel Ezekwo

Appendix E

A brief statement by High Chief (Engr.) Samuel Ezekwo at the Inauguration of planning committee for 2020 handover of catechist (Ide) Gabriel N. Ezekwo memorial chapel and Umuchu unity center to Auguata Diocese; and Ide Gabriel Ezekwo's biography book presentation on 14 December 2019.

Gentlemen, I thank you from the bottom of my heart for accepting my invitation to participate in this noble project – planning committee (PC) for handover of the renovated/rebuilt historic St. Thomas Stone Church, the Catechist (Ide) Gabriel N. Ezekwo Memorial Chapel and Umuchu Unity Center.

It is noteworthy that members of this PC are drawn from communities where Ide Gabriel Ezekwo served as teacher and catechist such as Nawfija, Uga, Ezinifite, Umuomaku, etc. Umuchu members of the PC are drawn from the Catholic church, Salvation Army, Anglican church, Evangelicals; and Umuchu Improvement Union Representative Assembly (UIURA).

As you know, this is one of the signature legacies of my late father and Umuchu people as a whole. And a symbol of love, peace, unity and community service "in the days" of the pioneers' generation.

I am happy to declare that the rebuilding of the

historic stone church is complete and it has been fully restored to its former glory.

Therefore, today, I officially inaugurate the PC for the grand opening and handover of this historic building to the Aguata Diocese.

This PC is hereby charged to articulate, and execute the following core objectives of the handover ceremony:

1 The ceremony shall showcase the stone church building as a symbol of love, peace, unity, and community service in Umuchu when all twelve Umuchu villages and religious denominations (including pagans) responded to Ide Gabriel Ezekwo's call and leadership to the successful execution and building of the historic stone church.

2 Life of Ide Gabriel Ezekwo (and his contemporaries – evangelists/pioneers in 1900s) shall be shown by reflecting on: In His Days, The Legacy of Ide Gabriel Nnolim "Ndigiri" Ezekwo (A Biography), which will be presented during the handover ceremony to encourage future generations to emulate them.

3 Members of the PC shall develop action plan to fully involve their respective constituencies in the ceremony by way of developing invitation lists from their constituencies; presentations, activities, tributes, etc. on the day of the handover.

4 The PC shall develop plans on how to reach out to far-away communities in southeast Nigeria where

Ide Gabriel Ezekwo served (that are not represented in the PC) so that they can actively participate in this noble project. Such communities are Amaraku, Amaimo, Amucha, Nkwere, Orlu, etc.

5 A sub-committee of the PC shall work with Venerable Obiagboso and the St. Thomas Perochial Church Committee to: (a) prepare evidence and documentation for application to list the historic stone building with United Nations Educational, Scientific and Cultural Organization (UNESCO). HRH Igwe G.O. Ezechukwu OON has graciously pledged to assist us in securing the coveted UNESCO status. (b) raise a Maintenance Committee (which shall be inaugurated at the handover ceremony) to manage the upkeep of the historic church building; (c) establish fees for rental of the building for conferences and functions; (d) establish rules and regulations guiding the use of the historic church building and funds generated by it henceforth.

Thanks for coming and may God bless you abundantly in return for your service.

High Chief Engr. Samuel I. Ezekwo
(Ide Umuchu)

Endnotes

1　K.O. Dike: 'Project Canterbury Origin of the Nigeria Mission 1841–1891'. A paper read at the centenary of the mission, held at Christ Church Onitsha on 13 November 1957. Ibadan University Press, 1962.

2　*Hertslet's Commercial Treaties, vol. III*, pages 18–19. Exhibited in 'Onitsha Market Crisis': Nnamdi Azikiwe, 1976, Zik Enterprises Ltd, Nsukka, Nigeria, page 52.

3　G.I. Jones: Dual Organization Africa, vol. 19 No2, 1942, in Igbo land before 1800, by A.E. Afigbo, Ground work of Nigeria History. Heinemann educational books PLC 1999, page 79.

4　Leo Nnoli: *The Culture-History of Umuchu from the Earliest Times to 1999*, Nolix Educational Publications, page 28.

5　Ibid, page 40.

6　Corbett Joe: The post-metaphysical meaning of soul and spirit in the cosmic mandala, www.integralworld. net/Corbett5.html.

7　Raymond Arazu: *Covenant Broken and Reconciliation (Sin in Salvation History)*, Liz Press Services Ltd Enugu, 1994, page 7.

8　G.O. Ezechukwu: *Autobiography*. Enugu, 2017, page 99.

9   An interview with Igwe Godson Ezechukwu, seventy-six years, retired public servant and paramount ruler of Umuchu, at his palace at Ugwuakwu village on 2 February 2017.

10 G.O. Ezechukwu: *Kingship Foretold: The Autobiography of Igwe Godson Ezechukwu*, Wisdom Ventures, Enugu 2017, page 22.

11 Leo Nnoli: op.cit. page 7.

12 www.iyienu hospital.50webs.org/history.htm

13 Rev. C.A Mbonu: 'The Coming of CMS to Umuchu (1916-1964)', in Maris Nkwo (ed.), The voice of Umuchu, vol 11 (maiden issue) December 1964, page 17.

14 E.A Afigbo: 'The Background to the Southern Nigeria Education, Education code of 1903', J.H.S.N vol 5, No 2 (June 1968), page 207.

15 K.B.C. Onwubiko: 'The Catholic Church and the development of Education in Eastern Nigeria (1885-1984)' in C.A., Obi (ed.)A Hundred Years Catholic Church in Eastern Nigeria: 1885-1985, (Nigeria: Africana Fep Publisher Ltd 1985), page 233.

16 B.A. Fafunwa: *History of Education in Nigeria*, London 1974, page 119.

17 Educational Policy in British Tropical Africa (London HMSO, 1925, CMD2374).

18 K.B.C Onwubiko: op.cit., page 232.

19 Report of the proceedings of the second session of the third synod of the diocese on the Niger, held in Port Harcourt on 30 April to 6 May 1938; published by CMS Niger Bookshop, Port Harcourt, page 65.

20 Ibid, page 81.

21 945 Report of the Onitsha Archdeaconry, contained in the synod of 1946, held at Onitsha 16 to 21 June 1946, printed and published by CMS Niger Bookshop. Port Harcourt.

22 Report of the proceeding of the second session of the first synod of the diocese on the Niger held at Port Harcourt, from 10 to 13 May 1932. DOIG Bros & Co. Ltd Heber Tower Press, page 6.

23 Ibid, page 10.

24 Report of the proceeding of the second session of the fourth synod of the Diocese of the Niger held on 10 to 16 May 1941, page 35 specifically recorded that Mr. G. Ikpeze was appointed as a travelling teacher who was stationed at Egbu but worked in schools within the entire Owerri district. This was an implementation of the proposal put forward by the manager of schools, Onitsha Archdeaconry, Michael Davidson, contained in the report of proceedings of the second session of the first synod, diocese on the Niger held at Port Harcourt 1932.

25 Biography of Chief Gabriel Nnoli Ezekwo contained in his burial brochure.

26 Chief Samuel Ezekwo: seventy-three years, during an interview with the author at his hometown in Umuojogwo village, Umuchu on 24 August 2019.

27 Synod report diocese on the Niger 1949, page 91.

28 Pa Eric Nwagboso: eighty-one years, chairman of Elders Council of Nawfija and former regent of Nawfija. Interview conducted on, 4 September 2017.

29 Anadi A.A.A. (edt): *Immanuel Anglican Church and Propagation of the Gospel in Ezinifite*, Aguata L.G.A (1916-1995). Ekwulobia, Nigeria. Pages 68 and 88.

30 Chief Luke Onwugamba, ninety-two years, describing Gabriel Ezekwo during an interview with the author on 3 March 2018.

31 Mishack Okwamanam Ezekwo: eighty-two years, retired church teacher. Interview conducted on 12 July 2017.

32 Umenweke et al (edt), *100 years of the Anglican Church in Umuchu (1916-2016)*, pages 21–22.

33 Ibid, page 28.

34 Venerable D.N. Obiagboso: archdeacon and vicar of St. Thomas' Anglican Church. Interview conducted at the church parsonage on 8 July 2017.

35 Address presented to the bishop of Awka diocese Rt. Rev. M.S.C. Anikwenwa on the occasion of the

dedication of Immanuel Church, Nwafija, 1 April 1991, at page 6.

36 Umeanulugwo Eleazer: seventy-seven years, retired teacher and first president of the Boys' Brigade in Immanuel Church Ezinifite. Interview conducted at the church premises on 23 July 2017.

37 Meeting proceedings of the appointment board, diocese on the Niger, held on 25 October. 1972, page 3, paragraph IV.

38 Anambra State Government Gazette: No31, Vol. 1 of 25 November 1976.

39 Deuteronomy 28, New King James Version (NKJV).

40 Leo Nnoli: op cit., page 198.

41 Samuel Ezekwo: narrating his discussion with his father in August 1990 during an interview with the co-author, at his country home in Umuojogwo village Umuchu on 24 August 2019.

42 Leo Nnoli: op. cit., pages 189–191.

43 Samuel Ezekwo: Relaying the speech of Igwe Ofobuike during his reception by Umuchu citizens resident in the USA.

44 T.O. Umeasiegbu: Umuchu, The Peace Restoration Efforts 1984–1986 of Archdeacon Mbonu Peace Committee Awka 2014. (Author's profile on back cover page).

45 Leo Nnoli: op. cit., page 174.

46 Posted letter to the Commissioner for Education and Information Enugu by the church council of St. Matthew's Catholic Mission Umuchu. Published in Igwe Godson Ezechukwu's Autobiography, Appendix 4, page 141.

47 G.O. Ezechukwu: op. cit., page 71.

48 Chief Frederick Nnanna Nnorom (alias Eziokwubundu I of Amaraku), eighty-eight years. Interview conducted at his residence in Amaraku-Amaise on 13 February 2017.

49 Ibid.

50 Pa Alford Ukaigwe, Secretary Dedication Planning Committee of Immanuel Church in 1991. During an interview with the author on 13 February 2017.

51 Umeanulugwo Eleazar: op. cit.

52 Augustus Nwakaife.

Bibliography

1945 Report of the Onitsha Archdeaconry, contained in the synod of 1946, Held at Onitsha 16 to 21 June 1946. Printed and published by CMS Niger Bookshop, Port Harcourt.

Achebe, Chinua: *There Was a Country: A Personal History of Biafra*. USA, 2012.

Afigbo, E.A: 'The Background to the Southern Nigeria Education, Education Code of 1903', J.H.S.N, vol 5, No 2 (June 1968).

Afigbo, A.E.: *Ground work of Nigeria History*. Heinemann Educational books PLC,1999.

Agbodike, C.C.: *Sources and Traditions of African Historiography* (Awka, 2004).

Anadu, A.A.A. (edt): Immanuel Anglican church and propagation of the Gospel in Ezinifite Aguata Local Government Area (1916-1995), 1995.

Anambra State Government Gazette: No31, Vol. 1 of 25 November 1976.

Arazu, Raymond: Covenant Broken and Reconciliation (Sin in Salvation History). Enugu Nigeria. 1994.

Arazu, Raymond: *Covenant Broken and Reconciliation (Sin in salvation History)*. Liz Press Services Ltd Enugu, 1994.

Arazu, Raymond: *Our religion – past and present*. Awka Nigeria. 2005.

Azikiwe, Nnamdi: *My Odyssey – An Autobiography*. Ibadan, Nigeria. 1970.

Azikiwe, Nnamdi: *Onitsha Market Crisis*. Nsukka, Nigeria. 1976.

Brands, H.W: *Reagan – The Life*. New York. 2016.

Clinton, Bill: *My Life*. New York. 2004.

Coleman, James: *Nigeria Background to Nationalism*. Sweden. 1986. US Library of congress catalog card No: 58-10286.

Corbett, Joe: The post-metaphysical meaning of soul and spirit in the cosmic mandala. www.integralworld.net/ Corbett5.html.

Crowder, Michael: *The Story of Nigeria*. Lagos, Nigeria. 1976.

Crowder Michael: *West African Chiefs: Their Changing Status Under Colonial Rule and Independence*. Ife, Nigeria. 1971.

Educational Policy in British Tropical Africa (London HMSO 1925, CMD2374).

Ekong, Sampson: *Evergreen Memories of Sir Louis Mbanefo*. Lagos, Nigeria. 2002.

Ezechukwu, G.O.: *Kingship Foretold: The Autobiography of Igwe Godson Ezechukwu Wisdom Ventures*. Enugu. 2017.

Ezeh, Ethel: *Archbishop Charles Heerey and the History of the Church in Nigeria (1890-2967)*. Mumbai, India. 2005.

Fafunwa, B.A.: *History of Education in Nigeria*, London. 1974.

Good News Bible. American Bible Society. New York. 1976.

Madiebo, Alexander: *The Nigeria Revolution and the Biafran War*. Enugu, Nigeria. 1980.

Mbonu, C.A: 'The Coming of CMS to Umuchu (1916– 1964)', in Maris Nkwo (ed.) The Voice of Umuchu, Vol 11 (maiden issue) December 1964.

Nnoli, Leo: The Culture-History of Umuchu from the Earliest Times to 1999.

Nweke D.C (ed.): From the Little Acorn to A Mighty Oak (A short History of St. James Church Enugwuabo). The Journey So Far. A compilation by centenary Planning Committee, 2011.

Obi, C.A.: *A Hundred Years of the Catholic Church in Eastern Nigeria: 1885-1985*, Nigeria. 1985.

Odinanwa, B.I.O.: *Nri People and the Spread of Their*

Tradition. Enugu, Nigeria. 1993.

Ojiakor, Ngozi and Unachukwu, G.C.: Nigeria Socio-Political Development (Issues and Problems). Enugu, Nigeria. 2001.

Report of the proceeding of the second session of the fourth synod of the diocese of the Niger held on 10 to 16 May 1941.

Report of the proceeding of the second session of the first synod of the diocese on the Niger held at Port Harcourt, from 10 to 13 May 1932. DOIG Bros&Co. Ltd Heber Tower Press, 53 Stone Wall Street.

Report of the proceedings of the second session of the third synod of the diocese on the Niger, held in Port Harcourt in 30 April to 6 May 1938; published by CMS Niger Bookshop, Port Harcourt.

Umenweke, M.N.: 100 years of the Anglican Church in Umuchu (1916-2016).

Umeasiegbu, T.O.: Umuchu – The Peace Restoration Efforts, 1984-1986 of Archdeacon Mbonu Peace Committee Awka 2014. Author's profile on back cover page).

Weigel, George: Witness to Hope, The Biography of Pope John Paul II (1920-2005). New York U.S Library of Congress Catalog card No. 99-26340.

www.iyienu hospital.50webs.org/history.htm

Unpublished Articles and Monographs

1 An address of welcome presented to his lordship, the
   Rt. Rev. Mis. C. Anikwenwa, by the entire people of
   Nawfija community on the occasion of the dedication
   of the Immanuel Church, Nwafija on 1 April 1991.
   Gabriel Ezekwo was identified as the twenty-fourth
   catechist of the church.

2 Burial brochure of Chief Gabriel Nnoli Ezekwo.
   1991.

3 Dike, K.O.: 'Project Canterbury origin of the Nigeria
   Mission 1841–1891'. A paper read at the centenary of
   the mission, held at Christ Church Onitsha on 13
   November 1957. Ibadan University Press. 1962.

4 Order of worship for centenary thanksgiving service,
   Umuchu Anglican community diocese of Aguata,
   held on 30 October 2016.

5 Posthumous award and order of thanksgiving
   service, Immanuel Anglican Church, Nawfija, held
   on 31 December 2017.

6 The History of the Church Missionary Society
   (CMS) in Osina (1916–2016).

7 Ukanwa Chioma G: Presidential address delivered
   at the 15 biennial mothers' union conference, 2017.
   Diocese of Isi Mbano, Owerri Ecclesiastical Province,
   held on 17 June 2017 at St. Peter's Archdeaconry
   Parish Amaraku.

Index

town union meetings 131–132, *see also* UIU (Umuchu
	Improvement Union)
traditions *see* Igbo communities

Printed in Great Britain
by Amazon